Zeronaire

Break Free from Income Dependency

By Paul Szyarto

Published by **PSG Publishing**
United States of America

ISBN (Paperback): 979-8-9944789-1-2

This book is intended for informational and educational purposes only. It is not financial, legal, or investment advice. The strategies and concepts presented are based on the author's experience and are provided for general guidance.

You should consult with a qualified financial advisor, accountant, or legal professional before making financial decisions. The author and publisher disclaim any liability arising directly or indirectly from the use or application of the information contained in this book.

First Edition
Printed in the United States of America

For those ready to remove the dependencies
that control their life.

**Every financial life has a structure.
Most people just don't see it.**

We'll help you find yours.

This book is designed to build.
Each section connects.
Each concept layers on the next.

You don't need to change everything at once.
And you don't need to believe that freedom requires more
money.

This isn't about cutting everything or living small.

It's about understanding what's quietly controlling your life,
and removing it.

Take this at your own pace.
Apply what resonates.
Return to what you need.

Freedom doesn't come from earning more.

It shows up when what you want no longer owns you.

Introduction: The Moment of Truth

The Financial Wake-Up Call

Let me say this as clearly as I can, because I've lived on both sides of it.

I've had the income. I've had the lifestyle. I've had the version of life that, from the outside, looks like you've made it. And I've also had the moment where I realized that none of it actually meant I was free.

That's the part nobody talks about.

When people look at success, they usually measure it by what they can see. The house, the car, the vacations, the way someone carries themselves. I had all of that at different points, and if you had asked most people, they would have said I was doing really well. And on paper, they weren't wrong.

But what wasn't visible was the structure underneath it all.

Every upgrade came with a new obligation. Every level up added another layer of responsibility. The house wasn't just a house, it was a number I had to hit every month. The cars weren't just cars, they were commitments. The lifestyle wasn't just something I enjoyed, it was something I had to maintain.

And once you build your life that way, something shifts without you even realizing it.

You stop working because you want to, and you start working because your life requires it.

That's a very different feeling.

It doesn't happen all at once. It builds slowly. You make a little more money, so you upgrade a few things. That feels justified. Then your income grows again, and your lifestyle follows it. Before long, you've created a version of success that looks impressive but is completely dependent on you continuing to produce at that same level.

There's no real margin. No real flexibility. No real ability to step back.

You can't just decide to take a break, or pivot, or slow down, because everything you've built is tied to your ability to keep earning. And the higher you go, the more pressure there is to stay there.

That's when it hit me.

I wasn't building freedom. I was building a very expensive version of responsibility.

And the hardest part to admit was this: I had done it to myself.

Not because I didn't know how to make money, but because I never stopped to question what my life actually required to run. I was focused on growing income, not reducing dependence on it.

That's the trap most people are in.

They think the answer is always more. More income, more growth, more success. And for a while, that works. It feels like progress. But if your obligations grow at the same pace as your income, nothing really changes.

You're just operating at a higher level of pressure.

That's why this book starts here.

Not with strategies. Not with investments. Not with how to make more money.

But with a simple question that most people never ask themselves:

Is your life designed for freedom… or is it designed to be maintained?

Because those are two very different things.

And once you see the difference, you can't ignore it anymore.

Your Numbers Don't Lie

Before we go any further, we need to do something most people avoid.

Not because it's hard… but because it's uncomfortable.

We need to look at your life in numbers.

Not your title.
Not your potential.
Not what you *could* be making.

Your actual numbers.

Because here's the truth, money becomes very real, very fast, when you stop thinking about it conceptually and actually write it down.

Start with your monthly income.

What actually hits your account each month after everything is said and done. Not your annual salary broken down in your head. Not your best month. The real, consistent number.

Now, we're going to do something even more important.

What does your life cost?

And I don't mean a rough guess like, "probably around five or six thousand." I mean the real number. The one that shows up whether you feel like working or not.

Mortgage or rent.
Car payments.
Credit cards.
Insurance.
Utilities.
Subscriptions you forgot you even signed up for.
Food.
Gas.
Everything.

When you add all of that up, what you're looking at is not just your expenses.

You're looking at your **required income**.

That's the number your life demands from you every single month just to stay exactly where you are. Not to get ahead. Not to invest. Not to grow.

Just to maintain.

Most people have never actually calculated this number. And if they have, they haven't really sat with what it means.

Because once you see it clearly, it changes how you look at everything.

That number is not just financial.

It's a reflection of your **dependency**.

It tells you how much of your life is already spoken for before you even start the month.

And here's where it gets real.

If your required income is high, you don't have as much freedom as you think you do.

It doesn't matter how much you make.

You can be bringing in a strong income, even a very strong one, and still be completely locked into it because your life is structured in a way that demands it.

I've seen people making great money who couldn't afford to slow down for even a few months.

Not because they weren't successful… but because their life had no margin.

Everything depended on the next paycheck.

That's when you realize something that most people never fully understand:

Income creates opportunity.
But obligations remove it.

And if you don't know your numbers, you don't know which one is actually running your life.

Your First Score

Now we take everything you just calculated and turn it into something most people have never actually seen before.

A clear measure of how dependent your life really is.

Not how much you make.
Not what you own.
Not how successful you look from the outside.

How much your life depends on what you earn.

Here's the formula:

Dependency Ratio = Required Monthly Income ÷ Total Monthly Income

That's it.

Simple, but brutally honest.

Take the number your life requires every month and divide it by what you actually bring in. What comes back is a number that tells you how much of your income is already committed before you even make a single decision.

And once you see it, it sticks with you.

If your number is around 0.80 or higher, most of your income is already spoken for. You are operating with very little flexibility. You might be doing well on paper, but in reality, you are maintaining a system that depends on you continuing to produce at a high level just to stay in place.

If you are closer to 0.60, there is still pressure. You have some room, but not much. A disruption, whether it is a job change, a slowdown, or an unexpected expense, starts to matter more than it should.

When you get down to around 0.40, things begin to change. You have options. You can absorb a hit. You can make decisions without everything tightening up around you.

And when you reach 0.25 or lower, you are in a completely different position. Your life does not demand much from you. You have space. You have flexibility. You can start making decisions based on what you actually want, not what you owe.

I remember the first time I calculated this for myself. I sat there longer than I expected to.

Because the number did not match the story I had been telling myself.

I thought I was doing well. I thought I had built something solid. And in a lot of ways, I had. But what that number showed me was that most of what I was earning was already committed before I even had the chance to use it intentionally.

I was not operating from choice.

I was operating from requirement.

That realization is uncomfortable, but it is also where everything starts to change.

Because once you see that your life is structured around a required number, you begin to understand something most people never fully grasp:

Freedom is not about how much you make.
It is about how much your life requires you to make.

That is the shift.

That is the moment things start to click.

And whether you like your number right now or not does not matter.

What matters is that you can see it.

Because once you can see it, you can change it.

And later, we'll flip this.

Because if this shows you how dependent you are, there's an inverse that shows you something far more powerful.

How free you can become.

Why This Book Matters

I didn't write this from theory.

I wrote this from experience.

I built a life that looked successful from the outside. The income was there. The lifestyle was there. By most standards, I was doing exactly what you're supposed to do.

But underneath it all, I realized something I couldn't ignore.

I wasn't free.

Everything I had built depended on me continuing to perform at that same level. The moment I slowed down, everything around me still expected to be fed. That's when it hit me.

I hadn't built freedom. I had built obligation.

And that realization forced me to ask a different question.

Not how do I make more.

But **why does my life require so much?**

That question changed everything.

It made me stop looking at my life based on what I could afford and start looking at it based on what it actually required to run. And once I saw that clearly, I started rebuilding it differently.

Less obligation. Less dependency. More control.

Over time, I got to a place where my life didn't need much from me to function. And for the first time, something showed up that I hadn't experienced before.

Space.

The ability to think clearly. The ability to make decisions without pressure. The ability to choose what I wanted to do with my time instead of being forced into it.

That's what this is really about.

This is not a book about becoming rich.

This is a book about getting your life back.

It's for the person who makes good money but still feels pressure every month.

It's for the person who looks successful on the outside but knows they can't step away.

It's for the person who is tired of the cycle of earning, spending, and maintaining.

And it's for the person who is starting to realize there has to be a different way to do this.

If that's you, this book is going to challenge how you think about money, success, and freedom.

It's going to show you where you actually stand.

And more importantly, it's going to show you how to change it.

Not through shortcuts. Not through hype.

But through a different way of thinking and a different way of building your life.

Because once you see this clearly, things start to shift.

And once they shift, you don't go back.

PART I – THE PROBLEM: The Income Dependency Trap

Chapter 1: The Debt Driven Economy

Section 1: Built on Borrowing

Most people think debt is a personal problem.

It's not.

It's a system.

And it's a system that works exactly as designed.

From the time you're young, you're trained into it without even realizing it. You're told to go to school, get good grades, and position yourself for a good job. Somewhere along the way, taking on debt for education becomes normal. Not just accepted, expected.

Then you graduate, start earning, and immediately step into the next phase.

You need a car. Financing is the easiest path.

You want a place to live. A mortgage is "just what people do."

You want to enjoy your life a little. Credit cards make that simple.

At no point does it feel like you're making extreme decisions. It all feels reasonable. Incremental. Even responsible.

That's what makes it so effective.

Because you're not pushed into debt all at once. You're guided into it step by step, each one justified by the stage of life you're in.

And before long, you're not just earning money.

You're managing obligations.

What most people don't realize is that the entire system is built to support this behavior. Banks make money when you borrow. Car companies make it easier to talk about monthly payments than total cost. Real estate markets are structured around what you can afford per month, not what you should actually take on.

Everything is framed in a way that keeps the focus on affordability, not ownership.

That distinction matters.

Because when you start thinking in terms of "what can I afford each month," you stop asking a much more important question.

Should I be taking this on at all?

And once you cross that line, it becomes very easy to keep going.

Upgrade the car. Increase the house. Add a few more subscriptions. It all fits, as long as the monthly number still works.

But that's the trap.

Because every new obligation may feel small on its own, but collectively, they start to define your life.

They determine how much you need to earn.
They influence the decisions you can make.
They limit how much flexibility you actually have.

And the system never pushes you to stop.

In fact, it quietly encourages you to keep going.

Because from the system's perspective, a person with no debt is not very profitable.

But a person with consistent payments?

That's predictable.

That's reliable.

That's ideal.

Which means the more you participate, the more the system rewards you for staying in it.

Better credit. Easier approvals. More access.

It feels like progress.

But what you're really doing is building a life that depends on you continuing to produce at the same level, month after month, year after year.

That's not accidental.

That's the design.

Section 2: The Normalization of Payments

At some point, the conversation changed.

It stopped being about what things cost…
and started being about what things cost **per month**.

That shift is subtle, but it's one of the most important changes in how people think about money.

You don't walk into a dealership and ask, "What's the total price?"
You ask, "What's the monthly payment?"

You don't look at a house and think, "Can I actually afford this?"
You think, "Can I make that payment work?"

Everything gets translated into a monthly number.

And once that happens, something important gets lost.

The **true cost**.

Because when you focus on the monthly payment, almost anything can feel affordable. Stretch the term out, adjust the rate, move a few numbers around, and suddenly something expensive feels manageable.

That's how people end up financing cars for six, seven, even eight years.
That's how people take on mortgages that quietly stretch their financial limits.
That's how subscriptions pile up without anyone really noticing.

Individually, none of it feels extreme.

Together, it becomes a system of constant outflow.

And here's the part most people don't stop to think about:

When you build your life around monthly payments, you're not just organizing your finances.

You're organizing your life around obligations.

Every payment becomes something that has to be covered.

Every month.

No matter what.

It doesn't matter how you feel. It doesn't matter if you want to take a break, try something new, or slow down for a while. The structure you've built doesn't adjust with you.

It stays fixed.

And that's where the pressure comes from.

Not from one big decision, but from a collection of smaller ones that all felt reasonable at the time.

A car here. A bigger place there. A few upgrades as income grows. It all makes sense in the moment. It even feels like progress.

But what you're really doing is locking in a required level of income.

And once that level is set, your flexibility starts to disappear.

You can't easily pivot.
You can't easily step back.
You can't easily say no.

Because everything is already spoken for.

The system reinforces this thinking, too. You're told to "build credit," to "leverage financing," to "take advantage of low monthly payments." And while none of that is inherently wrong, it all points in the same direction.

More commitments. More structure. More dependency.

It becomes so normal that most people don't question it.

They just assume this is how life works.

You earn, you spend, you manage your payments, and you repeat.

But when you step back and really look at it, you start to see something different.

A life built this way isn't designed for freedom.

It's designed to be **maintained**.

And once you see that clearly, it changes how you look at every decision moving forward.

Section 3: The Invisible Chains

The hardest part about debt isn't the interest.

It's the control.

And what makes it so dangerous is that you rarely feel it happening in real time.

There's no single moment where everything becomes overwhelming. No clear point where you stop and say, "This is too much." Instead, it builds gradually, one decision layered on top of another, each one reasonable on its own.

That's why it's so easy to miss.

You finance a car because you need transportation. You take on a mortgage because owning a home feels like the right move. You carry a balance for a little while because it helps smooth things out. None of those decisions feel reckless in the moment.

They feel normal.

That's exactly what makes them powerful.

Because over time, those individual decisions start to combine into something much bigger than any one of them. They create a structure that begins to define how you live, how you think, and what you can realistically do with your life.

What you end up with is not just a set of financial obligations.

You end up with a version of yourself that your life now requires.

A version of you that has to keep earning at a certain level. A version of you that has to keep showing up, performing, and producing, whether you feel like it or not. A version of you that starts to make decisions based less on desire and more on necessity.

That shift is subtle, but once it happens, it changes everything.

Instead of asking what you actually want to do, you begin filtering everything through a different lens. You start thinking about what you can afford to do without disrupting the structure you've built. You start weighing decisions based on risk to your income, not alignment with your priorities.

And over time, your world narrows.

Opportunities that once felt exciting begin to feel risky. Taking time off starts to feel irresponsible. Even small changes begin to carry more weight than they should, because your life is no longer flexible enough to absorb them easily.

This is where most people unknowingly get stuck.

Not because they lack ability or ambition, but because their financial structure limits their range of motion. They are capable of more, but constrained by what they've committed to maintaining.

And the system reinforces this way of thinking.

You're told this is what responsibility looks like. That this is the cost of success. That having obligations is a sign that you're doing things right. So you adapt to it. You accept it. You build around it.

I did the same thing.

Until I started to notice how often my decisions were being shaped by what I had already committed to, instead of what I actually wanted to do. That realization forced me to step back and look at my life differently.

Not based on how it looked.

But based on what it required.

Because once your life requires a certain level of income to function, you are no longer fully in control of your time. You are operating within a system that expects something from you, consistently, whether you want to give it or not.

That's what makes these chains invisible.

They don't feel like restrictions.

They feel like responsibility.

But the outcome is the same.

They limit your flexibility. They influence your decisions. They quietly reduce your ability to choose a different path, even when you know you want one.

And once you see that clearly, the question becomes impossible to ignore.

Are you building a life you actually control...

or one that controls you?

Chapter 2: The Illusion of Wealth

Section 1: Looking Rich vs Being Free

One of the biggest misconceptions people have about money is this:

They think they can recognize wealth when they see it.

A nice house, expensive cars, designer clothes, high-end vacations. From the outside, it all signals the same thing.

Success.

And for a long time, I believed that too.

I thought if someone had those things, they must be doing well. That they had figured something out. That they had reached a level most people were trying to get to.

But once I started getting closer to that world, and eventually living in it myself, I realized something that completely changed how I see all of it.

A lot of what looks like wealth… isn't.

It's financed.

It's structured.

It's supported by income that has to keep showing up every single month.

That's not always obvious from the outside. In fact, it's usually hidden behind the appearance of stability. Everything looks clean, controlled, and intentional. But underneath it, there is often a level of pressure that doesn't match what you see.

Because when your lifestyle is built on ongoing obligations, it doesn't matter how impressive it looks.

It still needs to be maintained.

And that creates a completely different reality than what most people assume.

You can have a high income and still feel stuck. You can have a great lifestyle and still have no flexibility. You can look successful and still not be able to step away for even a short period of time without everything tightening up around you.

That's when I started to separate two things that most people treat as the same.

Looking rich… and being free.

Looking rich is external. It's visible. It's what people can see and react to.

Being free is internal. It's structural. It's about whether your life actually allows you to make decisions without financial pressure dictating them.

And the two don't always align.

In fact, a lot of the time, they move in opposite directions.

Because the more you build your life around visible success, the more you tend to increase the level of obligation required to support it.

That's the trade most people don't realize they're making.

They're optimizing for appearance, not freedom.

And once you see that clearly, it changes how you look at everything.

Not just what people have.

But what it likely costs them to maintain it.

Section 2: The Lifestyle Illusion

Once you start seeing the difference between **looking rich** and **being free**, something else becomes clear pretty quickly.

A lot of what we call "success" is really just a **well-maintained lifestyle**.

And that lifestyle is often built on a very specific structure.

Income comes in.
Obligations go out.
Repeat.

As long as that loop keeps running, everything looks fine.

The house is paid for. The cars are covered. The trips happen. The upgrades continue. From the outside, it feels like progress. It feels like someone is moving forward, building something, leveling up.

But underneath it, the entire system depends on one thing.

Consistency of income.

The moment that slows down, everything else starts to tighten.

That's what makes it an illusion.

Because it gives the appearance of stability, but it's actually fragile. It only works as long as all the moving pieces keep moving in the right direction. And the more complex the lifestyle becomes, the more sensitive it is to disruption.

I've seen people with great incomes feel constant pressure because their lifestyle had no margin. Every dollar had a destination before it even arrived. There was no buffer, no flexibility, no real ability to adjust if something changed.

And that's when you realize something important.

It's not the lifestyle itself that creates the problem.

It's the **dependency required to sustain it**.

Two people can live in similar houses, drive similar cars, and spend similar amounts of money, but have completely different levels of freedom depending on how their life is structured.

One is choosing it.

The other is maintaining it.

That difference matters more than most people think.

Because when you're maintaining a lifestyle, you don't really get to question it. You don't get to step back and decide if it still makes sense for you. You're already committed. The system is already in place.

And over time, that system starts to shape your decisions.

You stay in situations longer than you should because walking away feels too disruptive. You avoid risks that might actually move you forward because the downside feels too expensive. You prioritize stability over opportunity, not because you want to, but because your structure requires it.

That's the tradeoff.

The lifestyle looks better.

But your range of motion gets smaller.

And the longer you operate like that, the more normal it feels.

You stop questioning it. You stop evaluating whether it's actually serving you. You just keep it going, because everything around you depends on it continuing.

That's why it's so easy to confuse lifestyle with progress.

Because as long as things are being maintained, it feels like you're doing well.

But when you step back and really look at it, the real question isn't whether your lifestyle looks successful.

It's whether it gives you any room to breathe.

Section 3: The Fragility of Image

Here's the part most people don't think about when they're building a lifestyle that looks successful.

How fragile it actually is.

From the outside, everything can look solid. The house is there, the cars are there, the routines are established, and it all feels stable. It gives off the impression that things are locked in and under control.

But a lot of that stability is conditional.

It depends on income continuing. It depends on things going according to plan. It depends on nothing significant changing.

And life doesn't work that way.

Income shifts. Markets change. Jobs evolve. Priorities change. Energy levels change. What once felt manageable can start to feel heavy, sometimes faster than expected.

When your life is built on a structure that requires constant input, even small disruptions start to matter more than they should. A temporary slowdown becomes stressful. An unexpected expense creates pressure. A change in direction feels risky, not because it is, but because your current setup isn't designed to absorb it.

That's where the illusion starts to crack.

Because what looked like strength from the outside starts to reveal how dependent it really is underneath.

I've seen people with impressive lifestyles feel completely boxed in the moment something shifts. Not because they weren't capable, but because everything around them was already committed. There was no room to adjust without affecting something else.

That's what fragility looks like.

Not failure.

Dependency.

And the more your identity is tied to how your life looks, the harder it becomes to acknowledge that fragility. You protect it. You maintain it. You keep it going, even when it no longer makes sense, because stepping away from it feels like losing something.

But what you're really protecting isn't freedom.

It's an image.

And that image comes at a cost.

It limits your ability to pivot when opportunities show up. It makes you more cautious than you should be. It keeps you focused on maintaining what exists instead of evaluating whether it still aligns with where you actually want to go.

Over time, you start to optimize for stability over growth. Not because that's what you want, but because your structure demands it.

That's the trade.

The stronger the image, the more fragile the foundation can become.

And once you see that clearly, the question shifts again.

Not whether your life looks solid.

But whether it can actually handle change without everything tightening around you.

Chapter 3: The Payment Lifestyle

Section 1: Monthly Life Design

Most people don't realize they've designed their life.

They think it just happened.

A few decisions here. A few upgrades there. A natural progression as income increases. It all feels organic, like things are simply evolving the way they're supposed to.

But when you step back and really look at it, there's a clear pattern.

Life gets structured around **monthly commitments**.

Not intentionally at first. It starts small. A car payment. Maybe a slightly higher rent or mortgage. A few subscriptions that feel insignificant on their own. Each one makes sense in isolation.

But over time, those individual decisions start to stack.

And eventually, they form a system.

A system where your life isn't just something you live.

It's something you have to **fund every month**.

That's the shift most people don't notice.

They're no longer thinking about the total cost of their life. They're thinking about whether they can make the monthly number work. And as long as that number feels manageable, everything else gets justified.

"I can afford it."
"It fits within my budget."
"It's only this much per month."

Those statements sound responsible.

But they're also what lock people into a structure that becomes harder and harder to change.

Because once your life is built around a certain monthly requirement, everything else starts to revolve around it.

Your income has to support it.
Your career has to sustain it.
Your decisions have to protect it.

It becomes the baseline you operate from.

And the higher that baseline gets, the less room you have to move.

You can't easily step back, because the number is still there. You can't easily pivot, because your life depends on maintaining it. Even taking time to think or reset starts to feel expensive.

That's when you realize something important.

You didn't just build a lifestyle.

You built a **monthly obligation system**.

And once that system is in place, it quietly starts dictating how you live.

Section 2: Subscription Living

At some point, ownership quietly disappeared.

Not all at once, but gradually.

Things you used to buy once and be done with turned into things you pay for every month. Music, software, entertainment, storage, security, services, even basic conveniences that didn't exist a few years ago. Each one feels small. Each one feels harmless.

But they add up.

And more importantly, they change how you experience your own life.

You're no longer just paying for big things like a house or a car. You're paying for access to everything around you. Your lifestyle becomes a series of ongoing agreements. As long as you keep paying, everything works. The moment you stop, things start to disappear.

That creates a very different relationship with money.

You're not thinking in terms of ownership anymore.

You're thinking in terms of **continuity**.

Can I keep this going?

That question starts to show up everywhere, even if you don't say it out loud.

You open your accounts and see a list of charges that just repeat. Some you recognize immediately. Others you barely remember signing up for. None of them feel significant on their own, but together they create a steady stream of outflow that never really stops.

And because it's spread out, it doesn't feel heavy.

That's what makes it effective.

If you had to write one check for the full cost of everything you pay for in a year, you'd probably pause. You'd question it. You'd reconsider a lot of it.

But when it's broken into smaller pieces and automated, it becomes background noise.

You don't feel it the same way.

You just maintain it.

Over time, this becomes your normal. Your life is no longer defined by what you own, but by what you are currently subscribed to. And maintaining that access becomes part of your financial baseline.

It's not optional anymore.

It's expected.

And once it becomes expected, it becomes required.

That's where the shift happens.

You move from choosing what you want to pay for to managing what you have to keep paying for. Your focus turns from intention to maintenance. You're no longer evaluating each expense based on whether it adds real value. You're just keeping the system running.

And the system keeps expanding.

New services. New tools. New conveniences. Each one designed to make life easier, faster, more efficient. And in many cases, they do. But they also increase the number your life requires every month to function.

That's the part most people don't track.

Not just how much they spend, but how much they've committed to continue spending.

Because every subscription, no matter how small, is another piece of your life that depends on ongoing income.

And when you stack enough of them together, you don't just have expenses.

You have a structure that quietly depends on you showing up and earning, over and over again, just to keep everything active.

Section 3: The Trap of Upgrades

Upgrades feel like progress.

You make a little more money, so you improve a few things. Maybe you move into a better place. Maybe you trade in your car. Maybe you start spending a little more on experiences, convenience, or things that make life feel easier.

On the surface, it all makes sense.

You worked for it. You earned it. Why wouldn't your life reflect that?

That's the logic most people follow.

And to be clear, there's nothing wrong with improving your situation. The problem isn't the upgrade itself. The problem is what usually comes with it.

An increase in obligation.

Most upgrades aren't one-time decisions. They come with a new baseline. A higher monthly number. A new level your life now has to sustain.

That's where things start to shift.

Because once you adjust to that new level, it doesn't feel like an upgrade anymore. It feels normal. It becomes your standard. And from that point on, maintaining it becomes the priority.

Then it happens again.

Income goes up. Lifestyle follows. Another upgrade. Another adjustment. Another increase in what your life requires.

It's subtle, but it compounds.

Before long, you're not just earning more.

You're **spending more to maintain more.**

And the gap between what you make and what you need doesn't expand the way you think it will.

That's the trap.

Most people believe that as their income increases, their freedom will increase with it. But if your obligations rise at the same pace, nothing really changes. You're just operating at a higher level with the same dependency.

I lived this.

Every time things improved financially, I justified raising the standard. Better house, better car, better everything. It felt like forward movement. It felt like I was building a better life.

But what I was actually doing was raising the cost of my life faster than I was increasing my flexibility.

That's a dangerous combination.

Because the higher your baseline gets, the harder it becomes to step back from it. You get used to it. You build around it. You start to assume it's necessary.

And once something feels necessary, it stops being a choice.

It becomes a requirement.

That's when the upgrades stop serving you and start controlling you.

You stay in situations longer than you should because the lifestyle needs to be supported. You avoid changes that might actually improve your life because the risk of disrupting your current structure feels too high.

And over time, you realize something that doesn't get talked about enough.

Not all progress is freedom.

Some progress is just a more expensive version of the same problem.

The real question isn't whether you can upgrade your life.

It's whether you can do it without increasing your dependency on income to sustain it.

Because if every step forward comes with a higher requirement, you're not creating freedom.

You're just making the system harder to escape.

Chapter 4: The Social Media Mirage

Section 1: Curated Success

At no point in history have people had this much visibility into other people's lives.

And at no point has that view been less real.

Scroll through any platform and it looks like everyone is winning. Nice homes, constant travel, expensive dinners, new cars, perfect moments captured at the right angle with the right lighting. It creates the impression that success is everywhere, and that you're either keeping up… or falling behind.

But what you're seeing isn't reality.

It's a highlight reel.

It's the best moments, filtered, edited, and presented in a way that tells a very specific story. A story of success, freedom, and lifestyle. What you don't see is what it takes to sustain it, or whether it's even sustainable at all.

There's no monthly breakdown under the photo. No explanation of what's financed, what's leveraged, or what's being carried in the background. You don't see the obligations, the pressure, or the tradeoffs that come with maintaining that image.

You just see the outcome.

And over time, that starts to shape how you measure your own life.

You don't compare your reality to someone else's reality.

You compare your reality to someone else's **presentation**.

That's an unfair comparison from the start.

Because you're measuring your full life, with all its responsibilities and constraints, against a version of someone else's life that has been selectively displayed.

But it doesn't feel that way when you're in it.

It feels like you're behind.

It feels like you should be doing more, having more, experiencing more. And that feeling, even if it's subtle, starts to influence your decisions.

You push a little further. Spend a little more. Upgrade a little sooner than you probably should.

Not because you need to.

Because it feels like you're supposed to.

That's the power of curated success.

It doesn't just show you a version of life.

It quietly convinces you that you should be living it too.

Section 2: Comparison Pressure

The problem with seeing everyone else's life all the time isn't just that it's curated.

It's that it creates a constant, low-level pressure to keep up.

Not in an obvious way. Most people aren't sitting there thinking, "I need to compete with this person." It's more subtle than that. It shows up as a feeling.

A feeling that you should be further along.
A feeling that you should have more.
A feeling that you're missing something.

And that feeling starts to influence your decisions, even if you don't realize it.

You start adjusting your standards based on what you see. What used to feel like enough doesn't feel the same anymore. What once felt like a good situation starts to feel average. And what used to feel like a stretch suddenly feels like the new baseline.

That's how comparison works.

It doesn't just change what you want.

It changes what you believe is normal.

And once your definition of normal shifts, your behavior follows.

You start spending in ways that align with that new standard. You justify upgrades earlier than you should. You make decisions not because they make sense for you, but because they feel aligned with where you think you should be.

It's not always dramatic.

In fact, most of the time it's small.

A slightly nicer car. A slightly bigger place. A few more experiences that feel like they match the level you think you're supposed to be at. Each decision feels reasonable on its own, but together they start to move your entire financial structure in a different direction.

Toward more.

More spending. More expectations. More obligation.

And the more you participate in that cycle, the harder it becomes to step outside of it.

Because now it's not just about what you want.

It's about how you compare.

You start to measure progress based on what you see other people doing, instead of what actually creates freedom in your own life. You lose sight of your own priorities, and replace them with a moving target that you don't control.

That's where people get stuck.

Not because they don't make enough, but because their expectations keep rising alongside everything they're exposed to.

I've been there.

You see enough of it, and it starts to feel like you should be operating at that level too. It doesn't feel like pressure at first. It feels like motivation. Like you're pushing yourself to do better.

But over time, you realize something.

You're not chasing your version of success anymore.

You're chasing a version that was never yours to begin with.

And that's a dangerous place to operate from.

Because when your decisions are driven by comparison, they rarely lead to freedom.

They lead to alignment with a standard that requires more from you than you probably intended to give.

Section 3: Buying Identity

At some point, spending stops being about what you need.

It becomes about who you are.

Or more accurately, who you want to be seen as.

That shift doesn't happen overnight. It builds over time, especially in an environment where everything is visible and constantly being compared. You start to associate certain things with certain identities. A specific type of car signals success. A certain neighborhood signals status. The way you travel, the places you go, even the brands you wear all start to carry meaning.

Not just to other people.

To you.

And once that connection forms, your purchases start doing more than serving a function.

They start telling a story.

"I'm doing well."
"I've made it."
"I belong at this level."

The problem is, that story often comes with a cost that isn't immediately obvious.

Because when you start buying identity, you're no longer evaluating things based on whether they make sense for your life.

You're evaluating them based on what they represent.

And that changes everything.

You justify things differently. You stretch a little more than you should. You convince yourself that it's worth it because of what it says about you, or how it positions you relative to others.

It feels like an investment in yourself.

But a lot of the time, it's an investment in an image.

And images need to be maintained.

That's the part people don't think about.

When your identity is tied to what you own, you don't just have to acquire those things. You have to keep them. You have to support them. You have to continue operating at a level that sustains that identity.

Which means your financial structure now has to support not just your life, but your **image of your life**.

That's where the pressure increases.

Because now stepping back isn't just a financial decision.

It feels like a personal one.

Downsizing feels like going backwards. Choosing something simpler feels like lowering your standard. Even making a smart financial move can feel uncomfortable if it doesn't align with the identity you've built.

I've felt that.

There's a moment where you realize that some of the things you thought you wanted… you actually just wanted to be associated with.

That's a hard thing to admit.

But once you see it, you start to separate two things that most people blend together.

What actually improves your life
and
what improves how your life looks

Those are not always the same.

And when you start prioritizing the second over the first, you begin building a life that is more expensive to maintain than it is valuable to live.

That's the trap.

Because the more your identity is tied to your lifestyle, the harder it becomes to change that lifestyle without feeling like you're losing something.

But what you're really losing… is the pressure to keep it going.

And once you understand that, you start making different decisions.

Not based on how something looks.

But based on whether it actually gives you more control over your life.

PART II – THE PSYCHOLOGY: Why People Stay Stuck

Chapter 5: Spending as Identity

Section 1: You Are What You Own

At some point, without anyone really saying it directly, most people start to tie what they own to who they are.

It doesn't happen all at once. It builds over time through what you see, what you're told, and what gets reinforced around you. Certain things begin to represent certain levels of success. A specific type of car signals that you've made it. A certain house means you're doing well. The brands you wear, the places you go, the way you live all start to carry meaning.

And eventually, that meaning becomes personal.

You're no longer just buying something because you need it or even because you want it. You're buying it because of what it says about you. It becomes a reflection of your progress, your status, and your position relative to other people.

That's where the shift happens.

Possessions stop being tools.

They become identity markers.

Once that connection is made, it changes how you evaluate everything. You don't just ask, "Do I need this?" You start asking, often without realizing it, "What does this say about me?"

That's a very different question.

Because now the decision isn't just functional. It's emotional. It's social. It's tied to how you see yourself and how you believe others see you.

And when purchases are tied to identity, they become much harder to challenge.

You don't easily walk away from something that feels like it represents who you are. You justify it. You protect it. You build around it.

I've done this.

There were things I convinced myself I needed, not because they added real value to my life, but because they aligned with the version of myself I thought I was supposed to be. And at the time, it felt completely reasonable.

That's what makes it so powerful.

It doesn't feel like overspending.

It feels like alignment.

But over time, you start to realize something important.

If your identity is tied to what you own, then your sense of self becomes tied to your ability to maintain those things.

And that creates pressure.

Because now it's not just about affording your life.

It's about maintaining the image of who you believe you are.

That's a heavy structure to carry.

And once you're in it, it becomes very difficult to separate what actually improves your life from what simply reinforces your identity.

That's where people get stuck.

Not because they don't make enough.

But because they've built a version of themselves that requires a certain lifestyle to support it.

And stepping away from that lifestyle starts to feel like stepping away from who they are.

That's the psychological anchor.

And until you see it, you'll keep making decisions that protect your identity, even if they limit your freedom.

Section 2: Status Signaling

Once possessions become tied to identity, the next step happens almost automatically.

You start to signal it.

Not in a loud or obvious way. Most people aren't walking around thinking, "I'm trying to show off." It's more subtle than that. It shows up in the choices you make, the things you prioritize, and the way you present your life to the outside world.

Because whether we admit it or not, people pay attention to signals.

They notice what you drive.
They notice where you live.
They notice how you spend your time and money.

And over time, those signals start to carry meaning.

So you begin to participate in it.

You choose things not just for how they function, but for what they communicate. A slightly nicer car than you need. A place that stretches your budget just enough to feel like a step up. Experiences that look as good as they feel.

None of it feels extreme.

In fact, it often feels justified.

Because you've worked for it. You've earned the right to enjoy it. And there's truth in that. The problem isn't the desire to enjoy your life. The problem is when enjoyment starts getting mixed with validation.

When part of the reason you're choosing something is because of how it will be perceived.

That's when spending becomes signaling.

And signaling creates a new layer of pressure.

Because now it's not just about making the purchase.

It's about maintaining what that purchase represents.

You can't easily step down without it feeling like a step back. You can't simplify without it feeling like a loss. You start to build your life in a way that needs to consistently reinforce the same message.

"I'm doing well."
"I've reached a certain level."
"I belong here."

That message has to be supported over time.

Which means your financial structure has to support it too.

And the more you participate in that cycle, the more it shapes your decisions. You become less focused on what actually creates flexibility in your life and more focused on what keeps you aligned with the level you've established.

That's where people lose control without realizing it.

Because the decisions feel small.

But the pattern is consistent.

You stretch a little more than you should. You justify things a little easier. You raise your baseline just enough that it becomes harder to step away from.

I've been there.

You tell yourself it's just part of success. That this is what moving forward looks like. And for a while, it feels like that's true.

Until you realize something that changes how you see it.

A lot of what we call success is really just **well-managed perception**.

And perception requires maintenance.

That's the cost most people don't calculate.

Because while signaling might elevate how things look from the outside, it often increases the level of obligation underneath it.

And once your life is built to support a certain image, it becomes much harder to ask a simple question.

Is this actually improving my life… or just improving how it looks?

Section 3: Emotional Spending

Not all spending is logical.

In fact, a lot of it isn't.

Most people like to believe they make financial decisions based on reason. That they weigh the pros and cons, think through the impact, and make choices that make sense.

But if you really look at how people spend, a lot of it has very little to do with logic.

It has to do with how they feel.

You've had the experience.

You have a long day. You're stressed, tired, maybe a little frustrated. You buy something small. It feels good. It gives you a moment of relief, a quick reset. Nothing major, just enough to change your state.

That's emotional spending.

And it doesn't stop at small purchases.

It shows up in bigger ways too.

You upgrade something because you feel like you deserve it. You book a trip because you need a break. You buy something new because you want a fresh start or a different version of yourself.

Again, none of this is inherently wrong.

The problem is when spending becomes a **tool for managing emotion**.

Because emotions are not consistent.

They change. They fluctuate. They react to everything going on in your life. And if your spending is tied to how you feel in the moment, your financial decisions start to become unpredictable.

You don't just spend when it makes sense.

You spend when it feels right.

And "feels right" is not always aligned with what actually supports your long-term freedom.

That's where people get into trouble.

Because emotional spending doesn't feel like a mistake when you're doing it. It feels justified. It feels earned. It feels like you're taking care of yourself in some way.

I told myself that more than once.

"This is fine."
"I deserve this."
"It's not that big of a deal."

And individually, it usually isn't.

But over time, those decisions add up.

Not just financially, but structurally.

Because every time spending becomes the response to a feeling, you reinforce a pattern. You teach yourself that the solution to discomfort, stress, or even boredom is to consume something.

And that pattern gets stronger the more you use it.

Eventually, it becomes automatic.

You don't even think about it. You just act on it.

That's when it stops being occasional and starts becoming part of how you operate.

And the more it becomes part of how you operate, the more it affects the structure of your life.

Because now your expenses aren't just tied to your needs.

They're tied to your emotional state.

That's a dangerous combination.

Because it creates a system where your financial behavior is driven by something that is constantly changing, and often outside of your control.

And over time, that leads to a life that costs more than it needs to.

Not because you lack discipline.

But because you never separated what you needed… from what you were using to feel better.

That's the shift that has to happen.

You don't eliminate spending.

You separate **intentional spending** from **emotional reaction**.

Because once you can make that distinction, you start making decisions that actually support your life, instead of just responding to how you feel in the moment.

Chapter 6: The Dopamine Economy

Section 1: Reward Loop

There's a reason spending feels good.

It's not random. It's chemical.

Every time you buy something, especially something new or unexpected, your brain releases dopamine. It's the same reward signal tied to anticipation, excitement, and satisfaction. It gives you a small boost, a quick lift, a sense that something positive just happened.

And your brain takes note of that.

It starts to connect the action with the feeling.

Buy something → feel better.

Do it a few times, and it becomes a pattern.

Do it enough, and it becomes a loop.

That loop is simple, but powerful. You feel a certain way, whether it's stress, boredom, or even just restlessness. You make a purchase. You get a temporary lift. The feeling passes. And without realizing it, your brain logs that sequence as something worth repeating.

The next time you feel that same way, the solution is already there.

Spend.

This is where it stops being about the item itself.

It's about the experience of buying it.

You're not chasing the thing. You're chasing the feeling that comes with it.

And that feeling is short-lived.

That's the part people don't talk about enough.

The excitement fades. The novelty wears off. Whatever you bought becomes normal faster than you expect. And once it does, the effect disappears.

So what do you do?

You repeat the process.

Another purchase. Another hit. Another temporary lift.

That's the reward loop.

And the more you rely on it, the more it shapes your behavior.

You start to seek out opportunities to buy, not because you need something, but because you want that feeling again. It becomes a subtle form of stimulation, something that fills space when nothing else is happening.

I've caught myself doing this.

Scrolling, clicking, adding something to a cart without really needing it, just because it felt like something to do. It didn't feel like a financial decision. It felt like a small, harmless action.

But over time, those small actions add up.

Not just in dollars, but in patterns.

Because once your brain gets used to that loop, it starts defaulting to it.

And that's when spending shifts from being intentional to being automatic.

The system around you is built to support this too.

Everything is designed to reduce friction. One-click purchases. Saved payment methods. instant approvals. You don't have to stop and think. You don't have to feel the cost in the moment. You just act, and the system handles the rest.

That makes the loop even easier to maintain.

Because there's nothing slowing you down.

No pause. No reflection. Just action and reward.

And the longer you operate like that, the more normal it feels.

You don't see it as a loop.

You see it as part of your routine.

That's when it becomes something you need to pay attention to.

Because once your behavior is being shaped by a cycle you're not consciously controlling, it's no longer just about money.

It's about how you're making decisions in your life.

And that's where things start to matter a lot more.

Section 2: Instant Gratification

The reward loop only works because it's immediate.

You feel something, you act, and you get a response right away. There's no delay, no waiting, no real friction between the impulse and the outcome. And that's exactly what makes it so effective.

Because the faster the reward, the stronger the behavior.

We've built a world where almost everything is available instantly. You don't have to save up for things the way people used to. You don't have to wait until you can truly afford something. If you want it, you can have it now, and figure out the cost later.

That changes how people make decisions.

You stop thinking in terms of long-term impact and start thinking in terms of immediate satisfaction. You ask yourself, "Do I want this?" instead of asking, "Does this actually make sense for my life?"

And in the moment, the answer is usually yes.

Of course you want it. Of course it feels like a good idea. That's how it's designed.

The cost is pushed into the background.

It gets broken into smaller pieces. It gets spread out over time. It gets framed in a way that feels manageable, even when the total impact is much bigger than it appears.

That's where short-term thinking takes over.

You make a decision based on how it feels right now, without fully accounting for what it creates later. And because the consequence isn't immediate, it doesn't carry the same weight in your mind.

You don't feel the future cost in the present moment.

So you move forward.

I've done this more times than I can count.

Something looks good. It feels justified. The monthly number works. You move on. No real hesitation, no deep evaluation. Just a quick decision that feels aligned with how you want to live.

But those decisions don't exist in isolation.

They stack.

Each one adds a little more to what your life requires. Each one slightly increases the baseline you have to maintain. And over time, that baseline becomes something you don't even question.

It just becomes your normal.

That's the trade most people don't recognize.

You get what you want now.

But you give up flexibility later.

And the more often you make decisions that prioritize the present over the future, the more your life becomes structured around maintaining those past decisions.

That's where instant gratification starts to cost you.

Not in one big, obvious way.

But in a slow shift toward a life that requires more from you than you originally intended.

And once that structure is in place, it's not easy to unwind.

Because now you're not just making new decisions.

You're carrying all the old ones with you.

Section 3: Addiction to Consumption

At some point, it stops feeling like a choice.

That's the part most people don't expect.

What starts as occasional spending, something tied to convenience or enjoyment, slowly becomes something more consistent. Then it becomes a pattern. And eventually, it becomes part of how you operate.

You don't think about it the same way anymore.

You just do it.

That's when consumption shifts from behavior to habit.

And habits, especially the ones tied to reward, are hard to break.

Because by now, it's not just about buying things. It's about the role spending plays in your day-to-day life. It fills gaps. It gives you something to look forward to. It creates small moments of excitement in between everything else.

Without realizing it, you start to rely on it.

You scroll, you browse, you click, you buy. Not because you need something, but because it's become a default action. It's something to do when you're bored, when you're stressed, when you're trying to shift your state.

And because each individual action feels small, it doesn't raise any alarms.

It feels normal.

That's what makes it dangerous.

Because when something becomes normal, you stop evaluating it. You stop asking whether it makes sense. You stop questioning the role it plays in your life.

You just continue.

I've caught myself in this cycle.

Not buying anything significant, just small things here and there. Something quick. Something easy. Something that felt like it didn't really matter. But over time, I realized it wasn't about the amount.

It was about the pattern.

The behavior had become automatic.

And once something becomes automatic, it starts shaping your life in the background.

Because now your spending isn't tied to intention.

It's tied to habit.

And habits don't care about your long-term goals. They don't consider your financial structure. They just repeat.

That repetition is what creates the real impact.

Not one purchase.

But the accumulation of hundreds of small, unexamined decisions that slowly increase what your life costs to maintain.

And the more your life costs, the more you have to earn.

That's how consumption turns into dependency.

It's not dramatic. It doesn't happen overnight.

It's a slow drift.

A series of small decisions that feel harmless in the moment, but collectively move you further away from flexibility and closer to obligation.

That's when it becomes something you need to step back and look at.

Not just what you're buying.

But **why you're buying it**.

Because once consumption becomes something you rely on to regulate how you feel or fill your time, it's no longer just a financial behavior.

It's part of your identity.

And until you see that clearly, you'll keep repeating it, even when you know it's costing you more than you want to admit.

Chapter 7: Social Comparison

Section 1: The Joneses Effect

Most people don't wake up and decide to compete with their neighbors.

It just happens.

You see what other people are doing. You notice how they live. The car in the driveway, the renovations, the vacations, the upgrades. None of it feels like pressure at first. It just registers.

But over time, it starts to shape your perception of what's normal.

That's the Joneses effect.

Not a conscious competition, but a quiet recalibration of your expectations based on what's around you.

What used to feel like enough starts to feel average. What used to feel like a stretch starts to feel reasonable. And before you realize it, your baseline has shifted.

You're not trying to outdo anyone.

You're just trying to stay aligned.

That's what makes it so subtle.

It doesn't feel like you're chasing anything. It feels like you're keeping up with what's expected at your level. Your environment sets the tone, and your decisions begin to follow it.

You upgrade because it feels like the next logical step. You spend because it fits the standard you now believe you should be at. You justify it because everyone around you seems to be doing the same thing.

And in that context, it feels normal.

I've experienced this firsthand.

You don't notice it while it's happening. It doesn't feel like a shift. It just feels like you're progressing, like you're moving forward with where you should be.

But when you step back and really look at it, you realize something.

You didn't define that standard.

You inherited it.

And once you inherit a standard, it becomes very easy to build your life around it without ever questioning whether it actually makes sense for you.

That's where people lose control.

Not because they're trying to impress anyone.

But because they've accepted a version of normal that requires more from them than they originally intended.

And once your version of normal gets expensive, your life starts to follow.

Section 2: Peer Pressure Economics

Not all pressure comes from social media or strangers.

A lot of it comes from the people closest to you.

Friends, coworkers, neighbors, people you spend time with regularly. The people you go out with, talk to, and naturally compare yourself to, even if you don't say it out loud.

Because money doesn't exist in isolation.

It exists in context.

And that context is often set by the people around you.

If your group goes out to expensive dinners, that becomes normal. If everyone upgrades their cars every few years, that becomes expected. If vacations, events, and lifestyle choices all sit at a certain level, you start to operate within that range without really questioning it.

Not because anyone is forcing you.

Because it feels like you belong there.

That's the part people underestimate.

It's not direct pressure.

It's alignment.

You want to participate. You don't want to be the one always saying no. You don't want to feel like you're operating at a different level than everyone else in your circle.

So you adjust.

Maybe just a little at first.

You stretch for a dinner you wouldn't normally justify. You say yes to a trip that feels slightly out of range. You upgrade something because everyone else has already moved to that level.

Each decision feels small.

Each one feels like it helps you stay connected.

But collectively, they start to shape your financial behavior.

Because now your spending isn't just based on your priorities.

It's based on your environment.

And environments are powerful.

They set expectations without saying a word. They create a standard that feels normal, even if it's higher than what actually makes sense for you. And the more time you spend in that environment, the harder it becomes to step outside of it.

I've seen this play out in both directions.

You can be around people who normalize overspending, constant upgrades, and living at the edge of your income. And over time, that becomes your baseline too.

Or you can be around people who value simplicity, control, and flexibility. And that shifts your perspective in a completely different way.

Most people don't realize how much influence this has.

They think their decisions are entirely their own.

But if you look closely, you'll see patterns that align almost perfectly with the people they're surrounded by.

That's peer pressure economics.

It's not about being told what to do.

It's about being surrounded by a standard that quietly influences what feels reasonable.

And once something feels reasonable, it becomes very easy to justify.

Even if it increases what your life requires to maintain.

That's where the trade happens.

You stay connected.

But you give up a little control.

And if you're not paying attention, that trade continues over and over again until your financial structure looks very different than what you would have built on your own.

Section 3: Invisible Competition

Most people don't think of themselves as competitive when it comes to money.

They're not trying to beat anyone. They're not keeping score in an obvious way. There's no leaderboard, no clear finish line, no direct comparison happening in front of them.

But the competition is still there.

It just isn't visible.

It shows up in small ways. You notice what someone else has and it registers. You see how someone is living and it sticks with you. You hear about a promotion, a purchase, a move, and it shifts something internally, even if you don't react to it outwardly.

You don't say anything.

But you adjust.

That's invisible competition.

It doesn't look like trying to win.

It looks like trying to stay aligned.

You don't want to fall behind. You don't want to feel like you're operating at a lower level than the people around you. So without realizing it, you start making decisions that keep you in that range.

You match pace.

Maybe not exactly, but close enough.

And because there's no direct comparison being spoken out loud, it feels like your decisions are independent. It feels like you're choosing what makes sense for you.

But if you step back, the pattern is clear.

You upgrade when others upgrade.
You spend when others spend.
You adjust your expectations based on what you see happening around you.

It's subtle, but it's consistent.

And over time, it creates a form of pressure that doesn't feel like pressure.

It feels like progress.

That's what makes it so difficult to recognize.

Because you're not reacting to one person.

You're reacting to a moving average of what everyone around you seems to be doing.

And that average tends to move in one direction.

Up.

More spending. More upgrades. More expectation.

Rarely less.

I've caught myself in this more than once.

Thinking I was just improving my situation, when in reality I was aligning with a level that had been set by what I was exposed to. It didn't feel like competition. It felt like growth.

Until I realized something.

If your decisions are being shaped by what other people are doing, even indirectly, you're not fully in control of the direction you're going.

You're being influenced by a standard you didn't set.

And that standard doesn't care about your long-term freedom.

It only reflects what's visible in the moment.

That's the problem with invisible competition.

There's no point where you win.

Because there's always another level.

Someone with more. Someone doing more. Someone showing more.

So the target keeps moving.

And as it moves, so does your baseline.

That's how people end up building lives that require more than they ever intended.

Not because they were trying to compete.

But because they didn't realize they already were.

And once you see that clearly, you start to ask a different question.

Not "Am I keeping up?"

But **"Is this direction actually mine?"**

Chapter 8: Financial Avoidance

Section 1: The Minimum Payment Illusion

One of the most effective ways people stay stuck is also one of the most common.

They focus on the minimum.

Minimum payment. Minimum due. Minimum required.

It feels responsible. It feels like you're handling things. As long as you're making the payment, you're doing what you're supposed to do.

That's how it's framed.

But that framing hides something important.

The system is not designed to help you get out. It's designed to keep you in.

Minimum payments are built to maintain the balance, not eliminate it. They're calculated in a way that keeps things manageable in the short term while extending the obligation over a much longer period of time.

So you stay current.

But you don't move forward.

That's the illusion.

Because as long as the number feels manageable, there's no urgency to change anything. You're not falling behind. You're not in crisis. Everything feels under control.

But underneath that feeling is a different reality.

You're maintaining the debt.

Not removing it.

And when you look at it over time, that becomes clear.

Balances move slowly, if at all. Interest accumulates in the background. What you thought would be temporary starts to stretch into something long-term.

And because it happens gradually, it doesn't trigger a strong reaction.

It just becomes part of your routine.

I've been there.

Looking at statements, seeing the minimum, paying it, and moving on. It felt like progress because I was staying on top of it. But in reality, nothing was changing.

The structure was still there.

The obligation was still there.

The dependency was still there.

That's the part the minimum payment hides.

It gives you the feeling of control without actually creating it.

Because real control doesn't come from keeping up with the system.

It comes from reducing your exposure to it.

And as long as you're operating at the minimum, you're still fully inside it.

That's why this matters.

Because if your strategy is built around maintaining the minimum, your outcome will be too.

And that keeps you exactly where the system wants you.

Active.

Engaged.

And dependent.

Section 2: Avoiding The Truth

Most people don't have a money problem.

They have an awareness problem.

Because if you don't fully see what's going on, you don't feel the need to change it.

And avoiding the truth is easier than most people think.

You don't open certain statements.
You don't total everything up.
You don't look at the full picture all at once.

You check just enough to feel like you're staying on top of things, but not enough to really understand what's happening.

That's not accidental.

It's uncomfortable to see the full number. It's uncomfortable to realize how much your life actually requires every month. It's uncomfortable to acknowledge how much of your income is already committed before you even make a decision.

So instead of confronting it, most people manage around it.

They look at pieces.

A balance here. A payment there. A quick glance at an account. Just enough to stay functional, but not enough to trigger a deeper evaluation.

That's how avoidance works.

It's not about ignoring everything.

It's about never putting it all together.

Because the moment you do, it becomes very real.

You see the total obligations. You see how much is going out. You see how much of your life is already spoken for. And once you see that clearly, it forces a different kind of thinking.

That's what people are avoiding.

Not the numbers themselves.

But what the numbers mean.

I've done this.

I've had moments where I knew, in the back of my mind, that things were tighter than they should be. But instead of sitting down and breaking everything out, I stayed at the surface level. It felt easier. Less pressure. Less urgency.

As long as nothing was immediately wrong, it was easy to keep moving.

But that's the trap.

Because avoidance doesn't stop the system.

It just delays your awareness of it.

The obligations are still there. The structure is still in place. The dependency is still operating in the background, whether you look at it or not.

And the longer you avoid it, the more normal it feels.

That's what makes it so dangerous.

Because you can live inside a structure that limits your freedom without ever fully acknowledging it.

You adapt. You adjust. You tell yourself it's fine because everything is still working.

Until one day, you realize you don't have as much flexibility as you thought you did.

And by then, the structure is already built.

That's why this matters.

Because you can't change what you won't fully face.

And the moment you actually sit down, look at everything, and understand what your life truly requires, you create something most people avoid.

Clarity.

And once you have clarity, you don't get to pretend anymore.

But you do get to change it.

Section 3: Living in Denial

Denial doesn't look like failure.

That's what makes it so easy to live in.

Most people think denial is obvious. They picture someone ignoring bills, falling behind, or clearly out of control. But in reality, denial is usually much quieter than that.

It looks like everything is fine.

The bills are paid. The accounts aren't overdrawn. Income is coming in. From the outside, nothing appears broken. From the inside, it feels manageable.

So you keep going.

That's denial.

Not because you don't know something is off, but because you've learned how to operate around it without fully confronting it.

You tell yourself it's temporary. You tell yourself things will get better as your income grows. You tell yourself you'll tighten things up later, when the timing is right.

Those stories feel reasonable.

They give you just enough comfort to keep moving forward without making any real changes.

I've told myself all of them.

"Once this next deal closes, I'll clean it up."
"Once income stabilizes, I'll start reducing things."
"This is just part of building something bigger."

And for a while, that logic holds.

Because nothing immediately forces you to change.

The system keeps running. The obligations get covered. Life continues at the same pace. And as long as that's happening, it's easy to stay in that space.

But what you don't see right away is what's building underneath.

The dependency increases. The required income rises. The margin gets thinner. And your ability to step back, pivot, or slow down continues to shrink.

Not suddenly.

Gradually.

That's the danger of denial.

It doesn't break you overnight.

It slowly locks you in.

And because it happens over time, you adjust to it. What once felt like a stretch starts to feel normal. What once felt temporary becomes permanent. You stop questioning it because you've adapted to it.

That's when you know you're deep in it.

When the structure no longer feels like a choice.

It just feels like your life.

That's where most people get stuck.

Not because they don't have options.

But because they've built a system that makes exercising those options feel too disruptive.

So they stay.

They maintain. They manage. They continue operating inside a structure that requires more from them than they would choose if they stepped back and looked at it clearly.

That's denial at its core.

Not ignorance.

Acceptance of a situation you haven't fully examined.

And the longer you stay there, the harder it becomes to see that anything needs to change.

Until something forces it.

And at that point, you're reacting instead of choosing.

That's why this matters.

Because if you catch it early, you still have control.

You can step back. You can evaluate. You can make changes intentionally.

But if you let it run long enough, the system starts making decisions for you.

And that's when you realize something you should have seen earlier.

You weren't just living your life.

You were maintaining a structure you never fully questioned.

PART III – THE CONSEQUENCES: The Cost of Income Dependency

Chapter 9: Payments = Future Time Sold

Section 1: The Time Conversion

Most people think they understand money.

They track it. They earn it. They spend it. They try to manage it the best they can. And on the surface, it feels like they have a handle on it.

But almost no one is actually looking at it the right way.

Because money isn't just money.

Money is time.

Every dollar you earn represents a portion of your life. Not in theory. In reality. It represents time you showed up, time you focused, time you gave your energy to something instead of something else.

That's the exchange.

You don't get paid in money.

You get paid for your time, and money is just how it's measured.

Once you really understand that, everything starts to look different.

Because now when you look at your income, you're not just seeing a number.

You're seeing how much of your life you're trading to generate it.

And when you look at your expenses, you're not just seeing what things cost.

You're seeing what they require from you going forward.

That's where the shift happens.

Take a simple example.

Let's say your take-home rate, after everything is said and done, comes out to about $50 an hour. That might not be exactly how you calculate it, but for the sake of understanding, it's close enough.

Now look at a $1,000 monthly payment.

On paper, it doesn't feel that heavy. It's just part of your budget. Something that fits into the structure you've built.

But translate it.

That's **20 hours of your life every single month**.

Not once.

Every month.

Year after year.

And that's just one payment.

Now start stacking them.

The mortgage. The car. The credit cards. The subscriptions. The things you've normalized because they were added gradually over time.

Each one takes a slice.

Each one pulls from the same place.

Your time.

When you add it all together, you start to see something that's hard to ignore.

A large portion of your future is already committed.

Not to things you're choosing in the moment.

But to decisions you've already made.

That's the part most people never sit with.

They look at their life as flexible, but it isn't as flexible as they think. Because before they even start their week, before they even decide what they want to do, a certain amount of their time is already spoken for.

They owe it.

To the structure they've built.

And the higher your obligations, the more time you owe.

That's the real cost.

Not the payment itself.

But the **time required to sustain it**.

And once you start seeing your life through that lens, it changes how you evaluate everything.

Because now the question isn't just, "Can I afford this?"

It becomes something much more real.

"Am I willing to give this much of my life for it?"

That's a different level of awareness.

And once you have it, it's very hard to go back to thinking in just numbers.

Because now you understand what you're actually trading.

Section 2: Selling Your Future

Once you understand that money is time, something else becomes very clear.

Every payment you commit to is not just a financial decision.

It's a decision about your future.

Because the moment you take on an obligation, you're not just dealing with today's money. You're committing future time, future effort, and future energy to something you've already decided to maintain.

That's what debt really is.

It's **pre-committed labor**.

You're agreeing, in advance, to show up and work a certain number of hours in the future to support something you chose in the past.

And most of the time, you don't fully think about it that way when you're making the decision.

You're focused on the present.

The car you want. The house that feels like the next step. The upgrade that seems justified. The experience that feels worth it.

All of that happens in the moment.

But the cost?

That lives in the future.

And it shows up in a way that's easy to overlook.

Not as one big payment.

But as a series of required actions.

Month after month.

Year after year.

You've already committed to it, so now your future has to adjust to support it.

That's the part people don't fully process.

Because when you make that decision, you're assuming something about your future.

You're assuming you'll have the same income.
You're assuming you'll have the same energy.
You're assuming you'll want to keep operating at the same level.

And sometimes, that holds.

But sometimes, it doesn't.

Your priorities change. Your interests shift. Your energy fluctuates. Opportunities come up that require flexibility. Moments happen where you want to slow down, step back, or go in a different direction.

And that's when the weight of those past decisions shows up.

Because now your future is already partially locked in.

You don't get to fully choose what to do next.

You have to consider what you've already committed to.

That's the trade.

You get something now.

But you give up a portion of your future flexibility in return.

I've felt this.

There were moments where I wanted to pivot, take a different direction, or simply create space. And on paper, it looked like I had the income and the success to do it.

But in reality, my structure didn't allow it.

Too much was already spoken for.

Too much of my future had been committed to maintaining what I had built.

That's when it hits you.

You're not just working for today.

You're working for decisions you made months or years ago.

And the more obligations you take on, the more of your future becomes predetermined.

That's what selling your future looks like.

Not in a dramatic way.

But in a series of quiet agreements you make with yourself that your future has to honor.

And once enough of those agreements are in place, your flexibility starts to disappear.

You're no longer fully choosing your path.

You're managing the one you've already committed to.

Section 3: The Hidden Cost

The obvious cost of debt is the payment.

The interest. The monthly number. The total you end up paying over time.

That's what people focus on, because it's visible. It shows up on statements. It's easy to calculate. It feels concrete.

But that's not the real cost.

The real cost is what it quietly takes from you over time.

Because once your time is committed and your future is partially locked in, there are things you lose access to without ever making a conscious decision to give them up. It doesn't feel like a trade in the moment. It just feels like the way life works.

It shows up in subtle ways at first.

An opportunity comes up, something that would normally excite you, but you hesitate. Not because it doesn't make sense, but because the timing doesn't feel right. There are too many obligations sitting in the background that need to be covered.

You tell yourself you'll revisit it later.

Sometimes later never comes.

It shows up when you need a break but can't fully take one. Even when you technically have the time, there's a constant awareness of what still needs to be maintained. The structure doesn't pause just because you do, so you carry it with you.

It shows up in decisions you don't even realize you're making.

You lean toward the safer option. You stay in situations longer than you should. You avoid risk, not because you lack confidence, but because your margin for error has been reduced by everything you've already committed to.

Over time, this creates a shift in how you operate.

You stop thinking in terms of possibility and start thinking in terms of protection.

You begin organizing your life around maintaining what exists, instead of evaluating whether it still aligns with what you actually want. You become more cautious, more calculated, more focused on stability than you ever intended to be.

And from the outside, it still looks like you're doing well.

That's what makes it so difficult to recognize.

I've been in that position.

On paper, everything looked strong. The income was there. The lifestyle was there. There was no obvious problem to point to. But internally, I knew there were limits. There were things I couldn't easily do, not because I wasn't capable, but because too much of my life was already accounted for.

Too many decisions had already been made.

That's when it starts to sink in.

Freedom isn't about what you have.

It's about what you can do without everything else being affected.

And when your life is built on a high level of obligation, your ability to do that shrinks in ways that aren't always obvious at first.

You can't easily step away without consequences. You can't easily change direction without disruption. You can't easily create space without something else tightening.

So instead, you adjust.

You work around it. You manage it. You continue operating within a structure that gradually reduces your flexibility, while still appearing stable on the surface.

That's the hidden cost.

It's not the payment.

It's the **loss of optionality**.

It's the slow narrowing of your choices.

It's the trade of freedom for maintenance, made one decision at a time until it becomes your normal.

And the longer you stay in that structure, the harder it becomes to even recognize what you've given up.

Until one day, you step back and see it clearly.

You didn't just build a life.

You built something that requires you to keep it running.

And that realization changes everything.

Chapter 10: The Career Trap

Section 1: No Exit

Most people believe they have options.

On paper, it looks that way. A solid resume, a good income, experience, connections. From the outside, it appears like they could make a move whenever they want. Change jobs. Take a break. Pivot into something different.

But when it actually comes time to make that move, something else shows up.

Hesitation.

Not because they don't want to leave.

Because they can't.

Or at least, it doesn't feel like they can.

That's the career trap.

It doesn't come from lack of opportunity. It comes from the structure built around your income. The more your life depends on that income continuing at a certain level, the harder it becomes to step away from it.

You start running the numbers in your head.

What happens if I leave?
How long could I sustain things?
What if the next move doesn't work out?

And those questions don't feel theoretical.

They feel immediate.

Because your obligations don't pause while you figure things out. They don't adjust to your transition. They stay exactly where they are, waiting to be covered.

That's what creates the pressure.

You're not just evaluating a career move.

You're evaluating whether your entire life can absorb that decision.

And in many cases, the answer is no.

So you stay.

Even when you've outgrown the role. Even when the work no longer excites you. Even when you know there's something else you'd rather be doing.

You stay because leaving feels too expensive.

I've felt this.

There were moments where I knew I wanted to shift direction. Not out of frustration, but out of clarity. I could see a different path that made more sense for where I wanted to go.

But when I looked at my structure, I realized something.

I didn't just need to make a change.

I needed to maintain everything I had already built while making that change.

And that's a very different situation.

Because now the decision isn't just about growth.

It's about survival.

That's the trap.

When your life is structured in a way that requires your current income to continue without interruption, your ability to make bold decisions disappears. You don't take risks that could move you forward because the downside feels too heavy.

So instead, you optimize where you are.

You adjust. You manage. You make the best of the situation.

And over time, that becomes your default.

Not because it's what you want.

Because it's what your structure allows.

That's when you realize something that's hard to admit.

You don't actually have as much freedom in your career as you thought.

You have a path.

And that path is being shaped by what your life requires, not just by what you want to do next.

Section 2: Income Dependency

At some point, income stops being a resource.

It becomes a requirement.

That's a very different relationship.

When income is a resource, you use it to build, to create, to move your life in a direction you choose. There's space. There's flexibility. There's a level of control in how you deploy it.

But when income becomes a requirement, everything changes.

Now it's not about what you can do with it.

It's about what happens if it stops.

That question sits in the background more than most people realize.

Because once your life reaches a certain level of obligation, your income isn't just supporting your lifestyle.

It's **holding it together**.

Every paycheck has a job before it even arrives. It's already allocated. Already spoken for. The margin between what comes in and what has to go out gets tighter, and over time, that margin becomes something you rely on staying consistent.

That's income dependency.

You don't just need to earn.

You need to keep earning at the same level, without interruption.

And that creates a form of pressure that doesn't always show up on the surface.

It's not panic.

It's constant awareness.

You start thinking in terms of continuity. Stability becomes the priority. Not necessarily because it's what you want, but because your structure demands it.

You begin to make decisions through that lens.

You stay in roles longer than you should because the income is predictable. You avoid moves that could increase your long-term upside because the short-term uncertainty feels too risky. You hesitate to take time off, even when you need it, because stepping away affects more than just your schedule.

It affects your system.

I've lived this.

There were points where income was strong, objectively strong, but the structure around it required that it stay that way. It didn't feel like leverage. It felt like responsibility.

Like everything depended on it continuing exactly as it was.

And that's when you realize something that most people miss.

High income does not automatically create freedom.

If anything, it can increase dependency if your obligations rise alongside it.

Because now you're not just earning more.

You're maintaining more.

That's the shift.

And once you're in it, it becomes very difficult to separate what you actually want to do from what you have to do to keep everything running.

Your decisions start to narrow.

Not because your options disappeared.

Because your structure filters them.

You start asking, "Will this disrupt my income?" before you ask, "Is this the right move for my life?"

That's a powerful constraint.

And over time, it changes how you operate.

You become more cautious. More focused on protecting what exists than exploring what's possible. You trade flexibility for predictability, not because you value predictability more, but because your system requires it.

That's the cost of income dependency.

It doesn't eliminate your ability to earn.

It limits your ability to choose.

And once your choices are limited by what your income needs to sustain, you're no longer fully in control of your direction.

You're maintaining a structure that depends on you continuing exactly as you are.

Section 3: Golden Handcuffs

This is where things get confusing for a lot of people.

Because from the outside, it looks like success.

High income. Strong title. Good benefits. A lifestyle that reflects years of progress. Everything most people say they want.

And yet, underneath it, there's a different reality.

Limited freedom.

That's what golden handcuffs really are.

It's not being stuck in a bad situation.

It's being stuck in a good one that you can't easily leave.

That's what makes it harder to recognize.

Because there's no obvious problem to point to. You're not struggling. You're not falling behind. In fact, by most standards, you're doing well.

But when you really look at your situation, you realize something doesn't fully add up.

You can't step away as easily as you thought.
You can't reduce your pace without consequences.
You can't take a different path without disrupting everything else you've built.

That's the constraint.

And it doesn't come from the job itself.

It comes from everything your life now requires that job to support.

The higher your income goes, the more opportunity you have to build flexibility.

But if your obligations rise with it, that opportunity disappears.

Now you're not just earning more.

You're responsible for more.

The house is bigger. The lifestyle is elevated. The expectations are higher. And all of it depends on you continuing to operate at that same level.

That's where the handcuffs tighten.

Because walking away isn't just a career decision.

It's a lifestyle decision.

And that's a much heavier choice.

I've seen this play out over and over again.

People who are highly capable, highly compensated, and outwardly successful, but internally feel constrained. Not because they lack options, but because their current structure makes those options difficult to act on.

They've built something that works.

But only as long as they keep showing up at full capacity.

That's the trade.

The income is strong.

But the flexibility is limited.

And over time, that creates a subtle but constant tension.

You start to feel it in small ways.

You think about stepping back, but you don't. You consider making a change, but you delay it. You recognize that you might want something different, but you stay where you are because everything around you depends on it.

It doesn't feel like you're trapped.

It feels like you're committed.

But the effect is the same.

Because commitment without flexibility becomes constraint.

That's what golden handcuffs really represent.

Not success.

But a version of success that requires you to keep it going.

And once you're in that position, the question becomes very real.

Are you building a life that gives you freedom…

Or one that depends on you maintaining it at all costs?

Chapter 11: Stress and Pressure

Section 1: Financial Anxiety

Not all stress is loud.

Some of the most damaging stress is quiet, constant, and always running in the background.

That's what financial anxiety feels like.

It's not always panic. It's not always tied to a specific event. It's a steady awareness that things need to keep working. That income needs to continue. That obligations need to be met, month after month, without interruption.

It sits with you.

You don't always think about it directly, but it shows up in how you operate. It influences your decisions, your mood, your energy. It creates a baseline level of tension that becomes so normal you stop noticing it.

Until it's gone.

That's when you realize how much of your mental space it was taking up.

Financial anxiety isn't just about not having enough.

It's about having just enough to keep everything going.

That's the part people don't talk about.

You can be earning well, covering everything, and still feel pressure. Because it's not about the current moment. It's about continuity. It's about what happens if something shifts.

That question is always there.

What if income changes?
What if something unexpected happens?
What if the structure I've built becomes harder to sustain?

Even if those things aren't happening, the possibility of them exists. And when your life is built on a system that requires consistency, that possibility carries weight.

So you stay alert.

You think ahead. You manage carefully. You try to keep everything balanced. And over time, that constant awareness starts to wear on you.

I've felt this.

Everything looked fine on the surface. Income was coming in. The system was working. But there was always a part of me thinking about what needed to be maintained.

It never fully shut off.

And that's the problem.

Because when part of your mind is always occupied with keeping your structure intact, it takes away from everything else.

Your focus is divided. Your energy is split. You're not fully present because something is always running in the background.

That's the cost of financial anxiety.

Not just the stress itself.

But the **mental space it consumes**.

And the longer you operate in that state, the more it becomes your normal.

You adapt to it. You function within it. You tell yourself it's just part of life.

But it doesn't have to be.

Because when your life requires less to maintain, that pressure starts to fade.

Not all at once.

But enough that you can finally feel the difference.

And once you experience that, you realize how much you were carrying without even recognizing it.

Section 2: Relationship Strain

Money doesn't just affect your bank account.

It affects your relationships.

And not always in obvious ways.

Most people think financial strain shows up as big arguments. Fights about spending, disagreements about priorities, tension around major decisions.

That does happen.

But more often, it shows up in smaller, quieter ways that build over time.

It's the conversations you avoid.
The purchases you don't mention.
The tension you feel but don't fully explain.

It's the moments where something feels off, but neither person wants to turn it into a bigger issue, so it just sits there.

That's how it starts.

Because when money is tight, or when your life depends on maintaining a certain level of income, it creates pressure. And that pressure doesn't stay contained to your finances.

It leaks.

It shows up in your tone. In your patience. In how you respond to things that normally wouldn't bother you. You become a little more reactive, a little less flexible, a little more guarded.

Not intentionally.

But consistently.

And over time, that affects the people around you.

I've seen this play out in subtle ways.

One person feels the weight of maintaining everything but doesn't fully express it. The other senses the pressure but doesn't understand where it's coming from. Small decisions start to carry more weight than they should.

A dinner becomes a discussion.
A purchase becomes a point of tension.
A plan becomes something to evaluate instead of enjoy.

And gradually, something that should be simple becomes complicated.

That's the effect of financial pressure on relationships.

It turns everyday decisions into loaded ones.

Because underneath them is a shared structure that has to be maintained.

And when that structure is tight, there's less room for flexibility.

Less room for spontaneity.

Less room for ease.

You start operating more like a system that needs to be managed than a relationship that gets to be experienced.

That's a subtle shift, but it matters.

Because relationships thrive on space.

Space to make decisions without overanalyzing them. Space to enjoy things without calculating the impact. Space to support each other without everything feeling like it carries weight.

When that space shrinks, tension grows.

Not always in a way that's visible.

But in a way that's felt.

I've been there.

There's a difference between making decisions from a place of freedom and making them from a place of constraint. And when constraint becomes the driver, it changes how you interact, even if you don't realize it at the time.

You become more cautious. More focused on keeping things stable than allowing things to flow naturally.

That's the trade.

The structure holds.

But the experience changes.

And over time, that can create distance.

Not because of one big issue.

But because of a series of small moments where pressure replaced ease.

That's why this matters.

Because money doesn't just impact what you can afford.

It impacts how you live.

And more importantly, how you connect with the people in your life while you're living it.

Section 3: Emotional Burnout

There's a point where the pressure stops feeling temporary.

It just becomes your normal.

You wake up, you move through your day, you handle what needs to be handled, and from the outside it looks like everything is working. You're productive. You're responsible. You're doing what you're supposed to do.

But underneath it, something starts to wear down.

Not all at once.

Gradually.

That's emotional burnout.

It doesn't come from one bad day or one difficult situation. It comes from operating inside a structure that constantly requires output, without giving you real space to recover.

Because when your life depends on consistent income, there's always something pulling on you.

There's always a reason to keep going.

Even when you're tired.
Even when your energy is low.
Even when you know you need a break.

You push through.

At first, it feels manageable. You tell yourself it's just a busy period. That things will slow down soon. That once you get past a certain point, you'll create space.

But that point keeps moving.

Because the structure doesn't change.

The obligations are still there. The expectations are still there. The requirement to keep producing doesn't go away just because you need rest.

So instead of stepping back, you adapt.

You lower your baseline. You accept that this is just how it is. You normalize a level of pressure that you would have questioned earlier.

That's where burnout takes hold.

Not in a dramatic collapse.

In a slow adjustment to a pace that isn't sustainable.

I've been there.

There's a difference between working hard and feeling like you have to keep working. When you're choosing it, there's energy behind it. There's purpose. There's a sense of control.

When you're required to do it, that changes.

It becomes maintenance.

And maintenance doesn't energize you.

It drains you.

Over time, you start to feel it in ways that are hard to explain at first. Your patience shortens. Your focus becomes harder to hold. Things that used to feel simple start to feel heavier.

You're still functioning.

But you're not operating at the same level.

That's the part people miss.

Burnout doesn't always stop you.

Sometimes it just reduces you.

You keep going, but with less energy, less clarity, less presence. You're doing the same things, but they take more out of you than they used to.

And because everything still depends on you continuing, you don't step back.

You keep moving forward.

That's the cycle.

Pressure leads to output. Output maintains the structure. The structure continues to create pressure.

And in the middle of that, your energy slowly gets depleted.

That's the cost.

Not just financially.

But personally.

Because when your life is built in a way that doesn't allow for real recovery, you're constantly drawing from the same source without giving it time to replenish.

And eventually, that catches up.

Maybe not in a way that forces you to stop completely.

But in a way that changes how you experience your own life.

Less enjoyment.

Less presence.

Less energy for the things that actually matter.

That's emotional burnout.

Not a moment.

A state.

And the longer you stay in it, the more it starts to feel like there's no other way to operate.

Until you step outside of it and realize there is.

Chapter 12: The Fragile Life

Section 1: One Shock Away

Most people think their life is stable.

The income is there. The bills are being paid. Everything is running the way it's supposed to. On the surface, it looks solid, like a structure that can hold.

But that stability is often more fragile than it appears.

Because for a lot of people, it depends on one thing continuing without interruption.

Income.

If that stays consistent, everything works. The system holds together. The obligations are met. Life continues at the level it's been built.

But if something interrupts that flow, even temporarily, the entire structure starts to feel different.

That's the reality most people don't test.

They assume stability because nothing has gone wrong yet. But they haven't actually looked at what would happen if something did.

Job loss.
Health issues.
Unexpected expenses.
A shift in the market.

None of these are extreme scenarios.

They're normal parts of life.

And when your life is built on a structure that requires constant input, even a small disruption can create pressure much faster than expected.

That's what makes it fragile.

Not that it's broken.

But that it depends on conditions staying exactly the same.

I've seen this happen.

People who were doing well, everything running smoothly, until something shifted. Not dramatically, just enough to interrupt the flow. And suddenly, the margin that felt comfortable disappeared.

Decisions that used to feel simple became stressful.

Time that used to feel flexible became tight.

Options that seemed available no longer felt realistic.

That's when the illusion of stability breaks.

Because what looked like strength was actually dependence on consistency.

And consistency is never guaranteed.

That's the part people don't fully account for.

They build their life based on what is happening now, without fully considering what happens if that changes.

And when you build that way, you're always closer to disruption than you think.

That doesn't mean something bad is going to happen.

It means your structure isn't designed to absorb it if it does.

That's the difference between stability and fragility.

Stability can handle change.

Fragility depends on avoiding it.

And once you see that clearly, you start to evaluate your life differently.

Not based on how well it's working today.

But based on how well it would hold if something unexpected happened tomorrow.

Section 2: High Income, Low Security

One of the biggest misconceptions people carry is that higher income automatically creates security. On the surface, that assumption makes sense. More money should mean more flexibility, more control, and a greater ability to handle whatever comes your way.

But in reality, it doesn't always work like that.

Because income, by itself, doesn't determine security. Structure does.

If your income increases but your obligations rise alongside it, the result isn't greater freedom. It's a larger system that now requires more to sustain. The numbers are bigger, but the dependency remains, and in many cases, it becomes even more pronounced.

That's where people get caught off guard.

They expect to feel relief as their income grows. They expect space to open up. Instead, they often find themselves managing a more complex version of the same situation. There are more commitments, higher expectations, and a greater number of things that depend on that income continuing without disruption.

I've experienced this firsthand.

There were points where income was significantly higher than it had ever been, and from the outside, it looked like everything should feel secure. By most definitions, it was success. But internally, it didn't translate into freedom.

It translated into responsibility.

Because the structure had expanded to match the income. The lifestyle had adjusted. The baseline had moved. What once felt like a stretch had become normal, and what became normal had to be maintained.

That's the part that changes everything.

When your life requires a certain level of income to sustain itself, your relationship with that income shifts. It stops being something you use to build your life and becomes something your life depends on to continue.

And that dependency creates pressure.

Not always in a dramatic way, but in a consistent, underlying awareness that things need to keep working. That income needs to remain stable. That disruption, even temporary, would have consequences that extend beyond the moment.

This is what creates the paradox of high income with low security.

From the outside, it looks strong. The numbers suggest stability. The lifestyle reinforces the perception of success. But underneath, the system is sensitive. It requires continuity. It depends on conditions remaining consistent.

And consistency is never guaranteed.

True security comes from having room within your structure. It comes from knowing that if something changes, you can adjust without everything tightening around you. It comes from having flexibility, not just in theory, but in practice.

When that room doesn't exist, the size of your income matters far less than people assume.

You can earn a great deal and still feel constrained. You can earn a great deal and still organize your decisions around protecting what you've built instead of expanding what's possible. You can earn a great deal and still hesitate when opportunities arise because your structure cannot easily absorb change.

That's the trade most people don't realize they're making.

They pursue higher income believing it will solve the problem, but if the underlying structure remains unchanged, the problem doesn't disappear. It evolves into something larger, more complex, and more difficult to step away from.

That's why income alone is not the solution.

Without control over your obligations, more income does not create freedom. It simply increases the level you are required to maintain.

Section 3: Managing High-Performance Seasons

For a long time, everything can feel like it's working.

The system runs. The income is there. The obligations are being met. From the outside, and even internally, it feels stable. You adapt to the pace, you manage the structure, and you tell yourself this is just how life operates at this level.

There's no clear breaking point.

That's what makes it so convincing.

But the truth is, the system only works as long as the conditions stay aligned. It depends on consistency. It depends on continuity. It depends on nothing meaningful interrupting the flow.

And eventually, something does.

It doesn't have to be dramatic.

Sometimes it's a shift in income. A role changes. A deal doesn't come through. A market tightens. Other times it's personal. Health, family, priorities, energy. Something that makes you step back, even briefly, from the pace you've been maintaining.

And in that moment, the illusion starts to break.

Because what once felt stable begins to feel tight.

The margin you thought you had starts to shrink. Decisions that used to feel routine suddenly carry weight. You begin to see how much of your life depends on everything continuing exactly as it has been.

That's when it becomes clear.

The stability wasn't structural.

It was conditional.

I've seen this happen, and I've felt it myself.

There's a moment where you realize that what you built doesn't have much tolerance for change. It works well in motion, but it doesn't handle disruption. It requires you to keep showing up at the same level, with the same output, just to keep everything intact.

And when that's no longer possible, even temporarily, the pressure shows up fast.

That's the breaking point.

Not necessarily collapse, but clarity.

You see the system for what it actually is. Not a foundation that supports your life, but a structure that depends on you to sustain it. And once you see that, it's hard to ignore.

Because now you understand the real risk.

It's not that something might go wrong.

It's that your life isn't designed to absorb it if it does.

That realization changes how you think.

You stop focusing only on how things look when everything is going well, and you start asking a different question.

What happens when they're not?

Can your life handle a slowdown?
Can it absorb a change in direction?
Can it function without requiring constant input?

If the answer is no, then what you have isn't stability.

It's performance.

And performance requires energy, attention, and consistency to maintain.

That's the illusion most people live inside.

As long as they can perform, everything holds together. But performance is not the same as freedom, and it's not the same as security.

Because both of those require something different.

They require a structure that can stand on its own, without depending on you operating at full capacity all the time.

That's when the shift begins.

Not when everything breaks.

But when you finally see that it could.

PART IV – THE ZERONAIRE PHILOSOPHY: Redefining Wealth

Chapter 13: The Zeronaire Equation

Section 1: The Core Formula

Most people measure success the wrong way.

They look at income. Titles. Net worth. What someone owns. What their life looks like from the outside. And based on those things, they decide whether someone is doing well or not.

That's how we've all been conditioned to think.

More income means more success.
More assets means more security.
More lifestyle means more progress.

But once you've lived through it, once you've built it and maintained it, you start to realize something that doesn't show up in those numbers.

None of that automatically gives you freedom.

You can have a high income and still feel locked in. You can have a strong balance sheet and still feel like you can't step away. You can build a life that looks successful and still feel like it depends on you continuing at the same level just to keep it going.

That's when you understand something most people never clearly define.

Wealth is not what you have.
Wealth is how much control you have over your time.

And once you look at it that way, you need a different way to measure it.

That's where the Zeronaire Equation comes in.

Freedom = Income ÷ Required Income

Simple.

But powerful.

Because it changes what matters.

It's not just about how much you make.

It's about how much of that income is actually required to sustain your life.

If your income is $200,000, but your life requires $180,000 to maintain, your freedom is limited. Your ratio is tight. There's not much room to move, adjust, or step back.

But if your income is $100,000 and your life requires $40,000, your situation is completely different.

Less income.

More freedom.

That's the shift.

Because now you're not measuring success based on the size of the number.

You're measuring it based on the gap between what you earn and what you need.

That gap is everything.

It determines how much flexibility you have. How much risk you can take. How much time you can reclaim. How easily you can step away, slow down, or change direction without everything collapsing.

I didn't fully understand this until I lived both sides of it.

I had periods where income was high, but so were the obligations. Everything depended on keeping that level going. On paper, it looked like success. In reality, it felt like maintenance.

Then I experienced the opposite.

Lower required income. Fewer obligations. More control.

And the difference wasn't subtle.

It was immediate.

Because for the first time, my time wasn't already spoken for before I even started my day.

That's what this equation captures.

Not how impressive your life looks.

But how much of it you actually control.

And once you start looking at your life through that lens, the goal changes.

You stop chasing more.

And you start creating space.

Section 2: Why Income Alone Fails

For most people, the solution seems obvious.

Make more.

That's the advice you hear everywhere. Increase your income, level up your career, build new streams, push higher. The assumption is that more income automatically leads to more freedom.

And in theory, it should.

If you earn more and keep everything else the same, you create space. You reduce pressure. You gain flexibility.

But that's not what usually happens.

Because as income increases, something else tends to increase with it.

Lifestyle.

You upgrade where you live. You upgrade what you drive. You upgrade how you spend. You start operating at a higher level because it feels like that's what the new income is supposed to support.

And over time, that new level becomes your normal.

That's where the problem shows up.

Because now your required income has risen alongside your actual income, and the gap that was supposed to create freedom never really forms.

You're earning more.

But you're also maintaining more.

I've lived this cycle.

There were times when income increased significantly, and it felt like things should open up. It felt like I should have more room, more flexibility, more control.

But that's not what I experienced.

Because each increase in income came with a corresponding increase in what my life required to sustain itself. The baseline moved. The expectations adjusted. What once felt like extra became necessary.

And once it becomes necessary, it stops creating freedom.

It creates dependency.

That's the part most people miss.

Income, by itself, doesn't determine your level of freedom. It only determines your potential for it. What actually determines your freedom is how much of that income you have to keep generating just to maintain your current life.

If that number is high, your dependency is high.

If that number is low, your flexibility increases.

That's why you see people at very different income levels experiencing completely different realities.

Someone earning $80,000 with a simple, controlled structure can have far more flexibility than someone earning $300,000 with a high-maintenance lifestyle.

On paper, it doesn't make sense.

In practice, it does.

Because the second person has less room to move.

Their structure requires continuity. It requires consistency. It requires them to keep producing at a high level just to stay where they are.

That's not freedom.

That's maintenance at scale.

And the more you build your life that way, the harder it becomes to step away from it.

You start optimizing for income stability instead of life flexibility. You make decisions that protect the structure instead of questioning it. You chase higher numbers, believing they will eventually solve the problem, without realizing that the structure is what needs to change.

That's why income alone fails.

Not because it isn't important.

But because without control over your required income, it doesn't do what you think it will.

It doesn't create freedom.

It just raises the level you have to maintain.

Section 3: The Shift

The shift isn't about earning less.

It's about needing less.

That's the part most people get wrong at first.

When they hear the idea of reducing required income, it can feel like stepping backwards. Like lowering your standard, giving something up, or not playing the game at the same level anymore.

But that's not what this is.

This is about control.

Because the moment your required income drops, something changes immediately.

You create space.

Not theoretical space. Real, usable space in your life. Space to make decisions without everything tightening around you. Space to step back without the entire structure depending on you continuing at the same pace.

That space is what most people are actually chasing.

They just think they'll find it by earning more.

I thought that too.

I kept pushing for higher income, believing that once I hit a certain number, things would open up. That I'd finally have the flexibility I was working toward.

But every time the number increased, the structure followed.

And the feeling didn't change.

The shift happened when I stopped focusing only on income and started looking at what my life actually required to function.

Not what I could afford.

What I needed to maintain.

That's a different question.

Because when you ask it honestly, you start to see things more clearly. You see what's essential. You see what's optional. You see what's adding real value to your life and what's simply there because it became part of your baseline over time.

And once you see that, you have a choice.

You can continue building around that structure.

Or you can start simplifying it.

That doesn't mean eliminating everything.

It means being intentional.

It means questioning whether each part of your life is worth the time it requires to sustain it. It means deciding what actually matters, and what you're willing to let go of in order to create more control.

Because every reduction in required income increases your freedom.

Every obligation you remove gives you back a portion of your time.

Every simplification creates flexibility that wasn't there before.

And the effect is not subtle.

It compounds.

You start to feel it in how you make decisions. You start to feel it in how you think about your time. You start to feel it in the way you approach opportunities, because you're no longer evaluating everything through the lens of what your life requires to maintain.

You're evaluating it based on what actually moves you forward.

That's the shift.

From maintaining a structure to designing one.

From chasing income to controlling requirements.

From building a life that depends on you to building one that gives something back.

And once you experience that difference, it's hard to go back.

Because now you understand something that most people spend years trying to figure out.

Freedom isn't found in how much you make.

It's created by how little you need.

Chapter 14: The Zeronaire Ratio

Section 1: Measuring Freedom

It's one thing to understand the concept.

It's another to actually measure it.

Because if you can't measure something, you can't really manage it. You can feel like you're making progress, but you don't know for sure. You don't know where you stand, and more importantly, you don't know how far you are from where you want to be.

That's why the Zeronaire Ratio matters.

It takes the idea of freedom and turns it into something you can actually see.

Zeronaire Ratio = Income ÷ Required Income

At first glance, it looks simple.

But when you apply it honestly, it becomes one of the most revealing numbers you'll ever calculate.

Start with your income.

Not what you could make. Not what you might make in a good month. What you consistently bring in, after taxes, in a way you can rely on.

Then calculate your required income.

This is where most people get uncomfortable.

Because required income is not your total spending. It's what your life actually needs to function at its current level. Housing, transportation, debt payments, insurance, essential expenses, and the lifestyle you've built that now feels non-negotiable.

Not what you think is reasonable.

What is actually required to maintain your current structure.

Once you have those two numbers, divide them.

And that's your ratio.

If your ratio is close to 1, it means almost everything you earn is already committed. There's very little room. Very little flexibility. Your life depends on you continuing at the same level.

If your ratio is higher, you have space.

A ratio of 2 means you earn twice what you need. That creates margin. It gives you options. It allows you to make decisions without everything tightening around you.

A ratio of 3 or more starts to feel very different.

That's where real flexibility begins.

Not because you're making an extreme amount of money, but because your life doesn't require most of it to keep functioning.

That's the key.

It's not about the size of your income.

It's about how much of it you actually need.

I remember the first time I looked at this honestly.

Not loosely. Not estimating. Actually breaking it down and seeing the real number.

It was eye-opening.

Because the gap between what I thought I needed and what I had structured my life to require was bigger than I expected.

And once I saw it, I couldn't ignore it.

That's what this ratio does.

It removes the story.

And replaces it with clarity.

And once you have clarity, you know exactly where you stand.

Not based on perception.

But based on reality.

Section 2: Interpreting Your Score

Once you calculate your Zeronaire Ratio, the number itself isn't the most important part.

What matters is what that number tells you about how your life is structured.

Because this isn't a score you compare to other people. It's a reflection of how much control you actually have over your time, based on the way your life is currently built.

If your ratio is close to 1, it means your income and your required income are almost the same. In practical terms, that tells you that nearly everything you earn is already committed. There's very little margin, and because of that, very little flexibility. Your life depends on consistency, and even small disruptions can create pressure faster than you might expect.

That doesn't mean you're failing.

It means you're operating inside a tight structure.

Most people live here without realizing it, because everything appears to be working. The bills are paid, the system runs, and nothing feels immediately broken. But underneath that, there's very little room to adjust, which is why decisions can start to feel heavier than they should.

As your ratio moves higher, things begin to change.

When you reach a ratio of 2, you start to create real breathing room. You're earning twice what your life requires, which means you have options. You can absorb changes more easily, you can make decisions without everything tightening around you, and you can start to think beyond just maintaining what exists.

At this level, you begin to feel the difference.

Not just financially, but mentally.

There's less pressure attached to every decision because your structure is no longer operating at its limit.

As the ratio continues to increase, the experience changes even more.

At 3 or higher, you're no longer just creating margin. You're creating flexibility that can be used intentionally. You can step back if needed, you can redirect your time, and you can evaluate opportunities without immediately filtering them through what your life requires to sustain itself.

That's where freedom starts to feel real.

Not because you've eliminated responsibility, but because your responsibilities no longer control every decision you make.

What's important to understand is that this progression is not about hitting a specific number and stopping. It's about recognizing where you are and what your current structure is allowing or preventing.

A lower ratio doesn't mean you're stuck forever.

It means your structure needs attention.

A higher ratio doesn't mean you've "made it."

It means you've created space, and now you have to decide how to use it.

That's the real value of the Zeronaire Ratio.

It gives you a clear, honest view of your position, without the noise of perception or comparison. It shows you whether your life is built for maintenance or flexibility, and it gives you a way to track your movement from one to the other.

Once you see that clearly, your decisions start to change.

Not because someone told you what to do.

But because you understand exactly what your current structure is costing you, and what creating more space can give back.

Section 3: What It Means for Your Life

The Zeronaire Ratio is not just a number.

It's a reflection of how your life actually operates.

Once you calculate it and understand where you stand, you start to see your decisions differently. Not in theory, but in real time. The ratio becomes a lens you begin to look through, whether you realize it or not.

Because now you understand something most people never fully quantify.

How much of your life is already committed.

If your ratio is low, your decisions are going to feel different. You're going to be more cautious, more calculated, more focused on maintaining what exists. Not because that's your personality, but because your structure requires it.

You might hesitate on opportunities that involve uncertainty. You might stay in situations longer than you should because the stability matters more than the potential upside. You might delay changes, not because they don't make sense, but because your life cannot easily absorb them.

That's not a mindset issue.

That's structural.

And once you see it that way, you stop blaming yourself for feeling stuck and start understanding why it feels that way.

As your ratio increases, your experience starts to shift.

You don't just have more money.

You have more control over how you use your time.

Decisions become less about protection and more about direction. You can evaluate opportunities based on where they could take you, instead of immediately filtering them through whether they will disrupt your current structure.

That's a completely different way to operate.

You start to notice it in small ways at first.

You feel less urgency around every decision. You're not constantly calculating whether something will "work" within your current setup. You begin to think longer-term, because you're no longer forced to prioritize immediate stability at the expense of everything else.

Over time, that compounds.

You take different kinds of risks. You say no more easily to things that don't align. You create space for things that actually matter, because your life is no longer filled with obligations that demand constant attention.

I experienced this shift.

There was a point where decisions started to feel lighter. Not because they were less important, but because they weren't all tied to maintaining the same structure. I could step back and think clearly, without everything being filtered through what I had to sustain.

That clarity is powerful.

Because once you have it, you start to design your life instead of managing it.

That's what this ratio ultimately gives you.

Not just a measurement, but awareness.

And awareness leads to better decisions.

Because now you understand the impact of each choice before you make it. You see how taking on a new obligation affects your ratio. You see how reducing something creates more space. You begin to evaluate everything based on whether it moves you toward more control or more dependency.

That's the shift.

From reacting to your structure to shaping it.

From living inside a system to designing one that works for you.

And once you start making decisions from that place, your life begins to change in a way that numbers alone can't fully capture.

Not because you have more.

But because you need less to live the way you actually want.

Chapter 15: Debt vs Leverage

Section 1: Destructive Debt

Not all debt is the same.

But most people treat it like it is.

They hear "debt" and think it's either good or bad, something to avoid completely or something to use freely. In reality, the distinction that actually matters is much simpler.

Does it create freedom?

Or does it reduce it?

That's the line.

Destructive debt is anything that increases your required income without increasing your control over time. It's debt that adds obligation without creating flexibility. It raises the number your life needs to sustain itself, and in doing so, it tightens your structure.

Most consumer debt falls into this category.

Cars that lose value but carry long-term payments. Credit cards used for lifestyle spending that extend beyond the moment they were used. Financing options that make things feel affordable in the present while quietly committing future time to maintain them.

Individually, these decisions often feel reasonable.

The payment fits. The purchase makes sense in the moment. The impact doesn't feel significant.

But over time, they stack.

And when they stack, they do something very specific.

They raise your required income.

That's the effect that matters.

Because every time your required income increases, your flexibility decreases. Your ability to step back, change direction, or absorb disruption gets smaller. You become more dependent on maintaining a certain level of income just to keep everything functioning.

That's the trap.

Destructive debt doesn't usually feel destructive when you take it on. It feels manageable. It feels justified. It feels like a normal part of building a life.

I've made these decisions.

Not out of carelessness, but because they made sense at the time. Each one had a reason. Each one fit into the bigger picture I was building.

But what I didn't fully account for was how they changed my structure.

They didn't just add cost.

They added requirement.

And requirement is what limits you.

Because once something becomes required, it stops being a choice. It becomes something your future has to support, whether it aligns with your priorities later or not.

That's what separates destructive debt from everything else.

It doesn't just cost you money.

It costs you flexibility.

And over time, that cost compounds in ways that are much harder to see than a simple balance or payment.

It shows up in the decisions you don't make.

The risks you don't take.

The space you don't have.

That's why this matters.

Because if your goal is to build a life with more control, more flexibility, and more ownership over your time, then any form of debt that moves you in the opposite direction has to be understood for what it is.

Not neutral.

Not harmless.

But something that quietly works against you if you're not paying attention.

Section 2: Strategic Leverage

Not all debt reduces your freedom.

Some of it, when used correctly, can increase it.

That's where leverage comes in.

Leverage is not about borrowing for the sake of having more. It's about using capital in a way that creates something beyond the cost of that capital. It's intentional. It's structured. And most importantly, it has a purpose tied to increasing your control over time.

That's the key difference.

Strategic leverage is not used to consume.

It's used to produce.

When you take on leverage the right way, the goal is simple. The outcome of that decision should either generate income, reduce your required income, or create an asset that gives you more flexibility in the future.

If it doesn't do one of those things, it's not leverage.

It's just debt.

That's where people get confused.

Because the same financial tool can be used in two completely different ways. One creates dependency. The other creates options. From the outside, they can look identical. Internally, they function in completely different ways.

I've used leverage in both ways.

There were times I took on obligations that didn't produce anything. They increased my required income and tightened my structure. At the time, they felt justified. Looking back, they limited me more than I realized.

There were also times where I used capital intentionally. To build something. To acquire something that created additional income. To put myself in a position where the output exceeded the requirement.

Those decisions felt different.

Because instead of adding pressure, they created space.

That's how you know you're using leverage correctly.

It doesn't just "make sense on paper."

It changes your structure in a way that gives you more control.

For example, if you take on debt to acquire something that produces reliable income, and that income exceeds the cost of the debt, you've shifted the equation. Your required income hasn't increased in the same way, because the asset is helping to carry the load.

That's leverage working for you.

Or if you use capital to build a system, a business, or a capability that reduces your reliance on a single income source, you've created optionality. You're no longer dependent on one path. You've expanded your range of motion.

That's leverage working for you.

But this only works if the outcome is clear.

If the numbers are realistic.

If the purpose is defined.

Otherwise, it becomes easy to justify decisions that feel strategic but function the same way as destructive debt.

That's where discipline comes in.

Because leverage amplifies outcomes.

If you use it well, it accelerates freedom.

If you use it poorly, it accelerates dependency.

There's not much middle ground.

That's why it has to be intentional.

Every time you consider taking on leverage, the question is not whether you can afford it.

The question is whether it improves your position.

Does it reduce your dependency?

Does it increase your flexibility?

Does it move you closer to controlling your time?

If the answer is no, then regardless of how it's framed, it's not leverage in the way that matters.

It's just another obligation.

And obligations, no matter how they're labeled, always come with a cost.

Section 3: The Decision Filter

Once you understand the difference between destructive debt and strategic leverage, the next step is applying it.

Because in real life, decisions don't show up labeled.

They don't come with a clear tag that says "this will create freedom" or "this will create dependency." Most of them feel reasonable. Most of them can be justified. And that's exactly why people get pulled into structures they didn't intend to build.

That's where the filter comes in.

Not a complicated system.

A simple way to evaluate every financial decision before you commit to it.

Because every obligation you take on is not just about money.

It's about what your life will require going forward.

The first question is the most important one.

Does this increase my required income?

If the answer is yes, you need to slow down.

Not stop.

But fully understand what you're committing to.

Because increasing required income reduces flexibility. It tightens your structure. It means more of your future time is already spoken for before you even get there.

If something increases your required income, it has to earn its place in your life.

That leads to the second question.

Does this create anything in return?

Not emotionally.

Structurally.

Does it generate income? Does it reduce another expense? Does it create an asset that gives you more control later? If the answer is no, then what you're taking on is pure obligation.

And pure obligation needs to be viewed clearly.

Because it doesn't just sit there.

It compounds.

The third question brings it all together.

Does this move me closer to or further from freedom?

That's the filter.

Simple, but honest.

Because once you ask that question without trying to justify the answer, things become very clear. You start to see which decisions are aligned with where you actually want to go, and which ones are pulling you in the opposite direction.

I use this filter now in ways I didn't before.

Not because I didn't understand money, but because I didn't always connect decisions to structure. I looked at whether something made sense in isolation, instead of how it would affect the overall system I was building.

That's where mistakes happen.

Because one decision rarely changes everything.

But a pattern does.

And patterns are built one decision at a time.

When you apply this filter consistently, something starts to shift.

You don't just react to opportunities or impulses.

You evaluate them.

You pause long enough to understand the impact, not just the immediate benefit. You become more intentional about what you allow into your life, because you know everything you add has a cost beyond the surface.

That doesn't mean you stop spending.

It means you start choosing.

Choosing what's worth your time.

Choosing what deserves a place in your structure.

Choosing what actually contributes to the life you want to build.

Because at the end of the day, every financial decision is also a life decision.

It either increases your control.

Or it reduces it.

And once you see that clearly, you stop asking "Can I afford this?"

And start asking something far more important.

"Is this worth a piece of my future?"

Chapter 16: The Four Financial Identities

Section 1: The Model

Most people don't have a clear framework for understanding how they operate financially.

They look at numbers. Income, expenses, net worth. But numbers only tell part of the story. What really drives financial outcomes is behavior. Patterns. The way decisions get made over time.

That's where the Four Financial Identities come in.

Not labels.

Not judgments.

A model.

A way to understand where you are, how you got there, and what it takes to move forward.

The progression is simple.

Spender → Borrower → Earner → Zeronaire

Each identity represents a different relationship with money, time, and control.

The **Spender** operates in the present. Money comes in and goes out with little structure. Decisions are driven by desire, convenience, and emotion. There's very little separation between what is wanted and what is purchased.

The **Borrower** takes it a step further. When income isn't enough to support the desired lifestyle, debt fills the gap. The structure expands beyond what is currently earned, and future time becomes committed to maintaining it.

The **Earner** has control over income. They can generate, grow, and sustain it. From the outside, this looks like success. And in many ways, it is. But if obligations rise alongside income, the Earner can still be highly dependent on maintaining that level.

The **Zeronaire** operates differently.

They focus on control.

Not just of income, but of required income.

They understand that freedom is created by the gap between what they earn and what they need. They design their life to keep that gap wide, protecting flexibility, optionality, and ownership of time.

This is not about perfection.

It's about awareness.

Because most people don't sit in one identity permanently. They move between them, sometimes without realizing it. They can earn like an Earner, spend like a Spender, and carry obligations like a Borrower, all at the same time.

That's normal.

The value of this model is that it gives you clarity.

It shows you the pattern behind your decisions.

And once you see the pattern, you can change it.

Section 2: Where You Are

Most people already have a sense of where they stand.

They just haven't defined it clearly.

Because when you look at your finances, it's easy to focus on the surface. Income looks good. Bills are covered. Maybe you're even saving or investing. On paper, things can appear solid.

But identity isn't about what it looks like.

It's about how it actually operates.

And when you step back and look honestly, patterns start to show up.

Not in one big decision, but in how you consistently behave.

You might see moments where you operate like a **Spender**. Decisions made quickly, based on how something feels in the moment. Little friction between wanting something and acting on it.

You might see patterns of a **Borrower**. Using future income to support current decisions. Carrying obligations that extend beyond what your current structure comfortably supports.

You might also see yourself as an **Earner**. Capable of generating income, solving problems, creating opportunities. From the outside, this looks like control, and in many ways it is.

But here's where it gets real.

You can be a strong Earner and still be highly dependent.

That's the part most people miss.

Because if your required income is high, your ability to earn doesn't automatically translate into freedom. It just means you're capable of sustaining the structure you've built.

And that's an important distinction.

The question isn't which identity you think you are.

It's which one shows up most often in your decisions.

That's where the truth is.

I've operated in all of them.

There were times I spent without thinking, times I borrowed to support a lifestyle, times I earned at a high level but still felt locked into maintaining it. From the outside, it looked like progress.

Internally, it didn't always feel like control.

That's when I started to see the difference.

Because identity is not about intention.

It's about behavior.

And behavior shows up in patterns.

If your spending is reactive, that's a signal.
If your obligations are growing faster than your flexibility, that's a signal.
If your income is high but your life still depends on it continuing without interruption, that's a signal.

None of these mean you're stuck.

They mean you're operating within a certain structure.

And once you can see that structure clearly, you can start to change it.

That's the purpose of this section.

Not to label yourself.

But to recognize your patterns without filtering them through how you want things to look.

Because once you're honest about where you are, you can finally make decisions that move you somewhere different.

Section 3: The Path Forward

Once you see where you are, the next question becomes obvious.

How do you move forward?

Not in theory.

In practice.

Because this isn't about jumping from one identity to another overnight. It's not about flipping a switch and suddenly operating like a Zeronaire. That's not how it works.

This is a progression.

And like any progression, it happens through a series of consistent shifts in how you think and how you act.

Most people try to change everything at once.

They cut aggressively, they overcorrect, they try to force a new structure immediately. And for a short period of time, it works. There's momentum, there's clarity, there's a sense of control.

But it doesn't last.

Because the underlying behavior hasn't changed.

That's why this has to be approached differently.

The path forward starts with awareness, but it moves through action.

Small, intentional changes that begin to reshape your structure.

If you're operating like a **Spender**, the first step is not restriction.

It's awareness.

You start noticing your decisions. You create space between impulse and action. You begin asking why you're spending, not just what you're spending on. That alone starts to change your pattern.

If you're operating like a **Borrower**, the focus shifts to control.

You stop expanding your obligations. You stabilize your structure. You begin reducing what your life requires, even if it's gradual. The goal is not perfection. It's direction.

If you're operating as an **Earner**, this is where the biggest shift happens.

Because this is where most people get stuck.

You already know how to generate income. You already know how to build. But now the focus is different. Now it's about protecting your flexibility, not just increasing your output.

You start questioning whether each decision increases your required income or reduces it. You stop assuming that growth automatically equals progress, and you begin evaluating whether that growth is actually giving you more control.

That's the turning point.

And as you move toward becoming a **Zeronaire**, the strategy becomes clear.

You simplify.

Not your ambition.

Your structure.

You reduce what is required. You eliminate what doesn't serve you. You become intentional about what you allow into your life, because you understand that everything you add comes with a cost beyond money.

Time.

Energy.

Attention.

And you start protecting those things.

I didn't make this shift all at once.

It happened over time.

It happened through decisions that didn't seem significant on their own, but collectively changed everything. Removing one obligation. Simplifying one area. Questioning one assumption.

Each step created a little more space.

And that space changed how I operated.

Because once you experience what it feels like to have control over your time, even in small ways, you start to want more of it. You begin to prioritize it. You begin to design around it.

That's how the identity shift happens.

Not through intention alone.

Through repetition.

Through consistent decisions that move you in the same direction.

Over time, those decisions stop feeling like effort.

They become your default.

And that's when you know you've changed.

Not because your life looks different from the outside.

But because it feels different from the inside.

You're no longer maintaining a structure that depends on you.

You're building one that works for you.

And that's the path.

Not to more.

To control.

And once you're on it, you don't want to go back.

PART V – THE ZERONAIRE SYSTEM: From Awareness to Control

Chapter 17: The Zeronaire Assessment

Section 1: Full Financial Inventory

Before anything changes, you have to see everything.

Not part of it.

All of it.

This is where most people struggle, not because it's complicated, but because it's uncomfortable. As long as you only look at pieces, things feel manageable. You can justify decisions, you can stay in motion, and you can avoid confronting the full structure you've built.

But the moment you lay everything out, the story changes.

Because now you're not guessing.

You're seeing.

And that clarity is what creates the opportunity to change.

The Zeronaire Assessment starts with a full financial inventory. Not just numbers on a spreadsheet, but a complete view of how your life is currently structured.

You're not just asking what you earn.

You're asking what your life requires.

That means listing everything.

Every fixed expense that shows up each month without question. Housing, vehicles, insurance, subscriptions, debt payments, utilities, recurring costs that have become part of your baseline. These are the things that define your required income, whether you think about them or not.

Then you look at variable spending.

What you spend on food, experiences, convenience, upgrades, things that feel optional but happen consistently enough that they've become part of your reality. This is where patterns start to show up, because what feels occasional is often far more consistent than you think.

Then comes the part most people skip.

Your obligations.

Not just what you pay, but what you've committed to.

Anything that requires future income to sustain. Loans, financing, long-term commitments, agreements you've made that your future has to support. This is where the weight of your structure becomes clear, because you start to see how much of your time is already allocated before you even get there.

And finally, you look at behavior.

Not just what you spend, but how you spend.

Do you make decisions quickly or intentionally? Do you justify things easily? Do you expand your lifestyle when income increases? Do you rely on future income to support current choices?

This is where the numbers connect to the psychology.

Because your structure didn't happen randomly.

It was built through patterns.

I remember the first time I did this honestly.

Not loosely, not estimating, but actually sitting down and laying everything out. Every obligation, every recurring cost, every commitment I had made.

It was more than I expected.

Not because I didn't know it was there, but because I had never seen it all in one place.

And once I did, something changed.

I stopped thinking about my life in terms of income and started thinking about it in terms of requirement.

That's the shift this section is designed to create.

Because until you see your full structure, you can't change it.

You can adjust around the edges. You can make small improvements. But you won't address the core issue, which is how much your life actually requires to keep running.

This isn't about judgment.

It's about clarity.

And clarity is where control starts.

Section 2: Identifying Patterns

Once you lay everything out, something starts to happen.

The numbers stop being the most important part.

The patterns take over.

Because what you're really looking for in this phase isn't just what you spend or what you owe. You're looking for **how you operate**. The behaviors that created your current structure and continue to reinforce it every day.

That's where the real insight is.

Because your financial situation didn't come from one decision.

It came from repetition.

When you step back and look at your inventory, certain things will stand out almost immediately. You'll see areas where spending is consistent, even if it felt occasional. You'll see obligations that were added over time, each one reasonable on its own, but collectively creating a structure that now requires more than you expected.

But beyond the numbers, you'll start to recognize your tendencies.

You might notice that you upgrade quickly when income increases. That as soon as there's more coming in, something expands to match it. That pattern alone can keep your required income rising indefinitely, even when your earning power improves.

You might see a tendency to justify purchases in the moment. Decisions that feel small and manageable individually, but form a consistent pattern when viewed over time. Not reckless, but reactive.

You might recognize reliance on future income. Commitments made with the assumption that things will continue as they are, or improve, without fully accounting for what happens if they don't.

These patterns are not random.

They're consistent.

And consistency is what builds your structure.

I've gone through this process myself, and what stood out wasn't the total number.

It was the repetition.

The same types of decisions, made in slightly different forms, over and over again. Each one made sense at the time, but together they created something I hadn't fully intended.

That's when you start to connect the dots.

Because now you're not just looking at what exists.

You're seeing what's creating it.

And once you see that clearly, you can start to separate two things that most people blend together.

Your situation
and
your behavior

Your situation is the result.

Your behavior is the driver.

That distinction matters.

Because if you only focus on the situation, you'll try to fix it at the surface. You'll cut a few things, adjust a few numbers, and for a while, it will feel like progress.

But if the behavior stays the same, the structure rebuilds.

That's why this step is critical.

You're not just identifying where your money goes.

You're identifying the patterns that determine where it will continue to go if nothing changes.

Once you understand those patterns, you gain something most people don't have.

Awareness with direction.

You know what to change, not just what to reduce.

And that's the difference between temporary adjustments and permanent control.

Section 3: Your Identity Result

At this point, you've done something most people never do.

You've laid everything out.

You've seen your full structure, and more importantly, you've identified the patterns that created it. Not just what exists, but how it got there.

Now it's time to connect it.

Because your identity is not something you choose.

It's something your behavior reveals.

When you look at your patterns honestly, one of the four identities will start to stand out. Not perfectly, not in isolation, but clearly enough that you can recognize where you spend most of your time operating.

You may see elements of the **Spender** in how quickly decisions are made or how often spending is driven by how something feels in the moment. That doesn't mean you are a Spender entirely, but it shows where control is being given up.

You may recognize the **Borrower** in the structure itself. Obligations that extend beyond what your current income comfortably supports. Commitments made with the expectation that future income will carry the load. That's not uncommon, but it is important to see clearly.

You may identify strongly with the **Earner**. You generate income, you solve problems, you create opportunities. On the surface, this looks like control, and in many ways it is. But if your structure requires that income to remain constant, then part of your identity is still tied to maintaining it.

And then there's the **Zeronaire**.

Not defined by income level.

Defined by control.

When you look at your structure and your patterns, the question becomes simple.

How much of your life is dependent on you continuing at the same level?

That answer tells you where you are.

I remember going through this process and realizing that while I saw myself as an Earner, a lot of my structure still reflected a Borrower. The income was there, but so was the dependency. That was a hard realization, but it was also the moment things became clear.

Because once you see your identity accurately, you stop operating based on assumption.

You start operating based on reality.

That's where change becomes possible.

This is not about labeling yourself.

It's about locating yourself.

Because you can't move forward if you don't know where you're starting from.

And once you know where you are, you can begin making decisions that move you in a different direction. Not randomly, not reactively, but intentionally.

That's the purpose of this step.

To take everything you've seen and translate it into clarity.

Not just about your numbers.

But about how you operate.

And once you have that clarity, the next steps are no longer abstract.

They're obvious.

Because now you're not guessing what needs to change.

You're looking directly at it.

Chapter 18: The Zeronaire Score

Section 1: Scoring Framework

Awareness is powerful.

But awareness without measurement doesn't last.

You can go through the assessment, see everything clearly, feel the impact of it, and still drift back into old patterns if you don't have a way to track where you stand and whether you're actually improving.

That's why the Zeronaire Score exists.

It takes everything you've uncovered and turns it into something you can measure, monitor, and improve over time.

Because what gets measured gets managed.

And what gets managed can change.

The Zeronaire Score is built around three core components.

Required Income
Obligation Load
Behavior Pattern

Each one represents a different part of your structure.

Required Income captures what your life needs to function. Not what you spend occasionally, but what is consistently required to maintain your current setup. This is the baseline that determines how much pressure your system creates.

Obligation Load looks at how much of your future is already committed. Debt, financing, long-term agreements, anything that requires future income to sustain. This is where time gets locked in before you even get there.

Behavior Pattern measures how you operate. Whether your decisions are intentional or reactive. Whether you expand with income or maintain control. Whether your actions consistently move you toward more flexibility or more dependency.

These three together tell the full story.

Because you can't look at just one.

You can have low required income but still operate reactively. You can have strong behavior but carry a high obligation load. You can be disciplined in some areas and completely unaware in others.

The score brings it all together.

Not to judge.

To clarify.

Each category is scored individually, and then combined into a single Zeronaire Score that reflects how your life is currently structured. Not how it looks, not how it feels, but how it actually operates.

I didn't have this framework early on.

I looked at individual pieces. Income, expenses, investments. But I didn't have a way to connect them into a single view of control.

Once I did, everything became easier to evaluate.

Because now I wasn't guessing whether I was moving in the right direction.

I could see it.

That's what this framework gives you.

A way to step back and evaluate your life objectively.

To see whether your structure is tightening or opening.

To understand whether your decisions are creating more freedom or reinforcing dependency.

And once you have that, you're no longer operating blindly.

You're operating with feedback.

And feedback is what allows real progress to happen.

Section 2: Your Current Score

Once you apply the framework, you get a number.

But the number itself isn't the point.

What matters is what it reveals about how your life is actually operating right now.

Because your Zeronaire Score is not a reflection of effort. It's not a reflection of how hard you work, how much you earn, or how responsible you believe you are.

It's a reflection of structure.

And structure tells the truth.

When you see your score for the first time, there are usually two reactions.

Clarity or surprise.

Sometimes both.

You might realize that your structure is tighter than you thought. That more of your income is committed than you were fully aware of. That your obligations are shaping your decisions more than you recognized.

Or you might see that you've created more space than you expected. That your structure has flexibility built into it, even if you haven't been fully using it.

Either way, the value is the same.

You're no longer guessing.

You're looking at reality.

That's what makes this step important.

Because most people operate based on perception. They feel like they're doing well, or they feel like things are tight, but they don't have a clear way to validate that feeling.

The score removes that ambiguity.

It shows you where you are on the spectrum.

Not in a general sense.

Specifically.

It shows you how much of your life is committed. It shows you how dependent your structure is on your current income. It shows you whether your behavior is reinforcing that structure or working against it.

That level of clarity can be uncomfortable.

Because once you see it, you can't unsee it.

But it's also what creates the opportunity to change.

I remember going through this process and realizing that while I thought I had control, a large portion of my structure was still dependent on maintaining a certain level of output.

It didn't feel that way day to day.

But when I saw it laid out, it was clear.

That's the power of this step.

It replaces assumption with evidence.

And once you have that, your decisions start to shift.

Not because you're trying to force change.

Because you understand what your current structure is actually doing.

You start to see how each decision affects your score. How taking on a new obligation moves it in one direction. How reducing something moves it in another.

It becomes tangible.

That's what most people are missing.

Not effort.

Feedback.

And once you have feedback, progress becomes something you can track.

Not just something you hope is happening.

Section 3: Improving Your Score

Once you know your score, the instinct is to fix everything at once.

That's where most people go wrong.

Because this isn't about dramatic change.

It's about directional change.

Your Zeronaire Score improves when your structure improves, and your structure improves through consistent, intentional decisions that shift how your life operates over time.

Not overnight.

The goal is simple.

Reduce what your life requires.
Improve how you operate.
Increase your control.

Everything else flows from that.

The first place to focus is required income.

Not by eliminating everything, but by questioning what is actually necessary. You start identifying which parts of your life are fixed because they need to be, and which parts are fixed because they were never re-evaluated.

There's a difference.

Some expenses support your life.

Others support a version of your life you've grown used to.

And once you see that clearly, you can begin to make adjustments that lower your baseline without feeling like you're sacrificing something essential.

Even small reductions matter.

Because every dollar you remove from required income increases your flexibility.

The second focus is obligation load.

This is where your future is tied up.

The objective here is not to panic or aggressively eliminate everything at once. It's to stop adding new obligations while systematically reducing existing ones.

You stabilize first.

Then you unwind.

Because as your obligations decrease, your future starts to open up. Less of your time is pre-committed. More of your decisions become optional again.

That shift is powerful.

The third focus is behavior.

This is where everything either holds or changes.

Because if your behavior doesn't shift, your structure will rebuild itself, even if you improve it temporarily.

You begin creating space between impulse and action. You evaluate decisions based on their impact on your structure, not just whether they feel justified in the moment. You stop expanding automatically when income increases, and instead decide intentionally whether something deserves a place in your life.

That's where control is built.

Not in one decision.

In repetition.

I didn't improve my structure all at once.

It happened through consistent adjustments.

Removing one obligation. Reducing one expense. Changing how I approached decisions. Each step created a little more space, and that space changed how I operated moving forward.

That's how the score improves.

Not through intensity.

Through consistency.

And as it improves, something else happens.

Your decisions get easier.

Because you're no longer trying to maintain a structure that requires constant effort. You're building one that supports you instead of depending on you.

That's the direction.

You're not chasing a perfect score.

You're creating a life with more room, more flexibility, and more control over your time.

And every step in that direction matters.

Chapter 19: The Zeronaire Playbook

Section 1: Eliminate

This is where things start to get real.

Up to this point, you've built awareness. You've seen your structure, understood your patterns, and measured where you stand. Now it's time to act.

And the first step is not optimizing.

It's eliminating.

Because before you can build anything better, you have to remove what's actively working against you.

That means identifying **destructive debt** and taking direct action on it.

Not all at once.

But intentionally.

Destructive debt is anything that increases your required income without creating value in return. It doesn't generate income. It doesn't reduce future obligations. It doesn't give you flexibility.

It just sits there.

Requiring time.

Every month.

That's what you're targeting here.

You start by listing it clearly.

Credit cards tied to lifestyle spending.
Financed purchases that no longer serve a real purpose.
Obligations that were justified in the moment but now just exist as part of your baseline.

You're not judging yourself.

You're identifying what needs to go.

Then you prioritize.

Not based on emotion, but based on impact.

Which obligations are increasing your required income the most? Which ones are costing you the most in terms of time and flexibility? Which ones, if removed, would immediately create space?

That's where you start.

Because elimination is about momentum.

You remove something, and you feel it.

Not just financially, but structurally.

Your required income drops. Your pressure decreases. Your flexibility increases. And once you experience that shift, even in a small way, it changes how you approach everything else.

I remember the first time I removed a meaningful obligation.

Not reduced it.

Eliminated it.

The difference was immediate.

It wasn't just the payment disappearing. It was the realization that something no longer had a claim on my future. That a portion of my time was no longer pre-committed to maintaining it.

That feeling matters.

Because it reinforces the direction.

This phase requires discipline.

Not extreme action.

Consistent action.

You stop adding new destructive debt. You redirect resources toward removing existing obligations. You make decisions that support unwinding the structure instead of expanding it.

And over time, it compounds.

Each elimination creates space.

Each piece of space gives you more control.

And that control is what you're building toward.

Because once you remove what's working against you, you create the foundation for everything that comes next.

This isn't about restriction.

It's about **removal of constraint**.

And once you start experiencing that, the motivation to continue doesn't come from discipline alone.

It comes from clarity.

You begin to see exactly what each decision is costing you.

And exactly what removing it gives back.

Section 2: Reduce

Once you've started eliminating what's clearly working against you, the next step is to look at what remains.

Not everything needs to be removed.

But a lot of it can be **reduced**.

This is where you begin reshaping your structure in a more precise way. You're not cutting randomly or reacting emotionally. You're evaluating what your life actually requires and adjusting it so that it demands less from you over time.

Because the goal is not to strip everything down.

The goal is to **lower your required income without lowering the quality of your life**.

That distinction matters.

Most people assume that reducing expenses means sacrificing something meaningful. In reality, much of what people maintain is not essential. It's simply familiar. It became part of the baseline, and over time, it stopped being questioned.

That's what you're addressing here.

You start with your fixed expenses.

Housing, transportation, recurring services, anything that shows up every month without a decision being made. These are the most important, because they define your baseline. Even small adjustments here create lasting impact, because they don't just happen once.

They repeat.

That's where leverage exists in reduction.

A lower housing cost. A different vehicle decision. Removing or consolidating recurring services that no longer add real value. These changes might not feel dramatic in the moment, but over time they reshape what your life requires to function.

And that's what creates space.

Then you look at variable spending.

Not to eliminate it, but to understand it.

Where are you spending out of habit instead of intention? Where are you maintaining patterns that don't actually improve your life, but have simply become routine? Where are you defaulting to convenience when there are alternatives that would reduce your baseline without reducing your experience?

This is where awareness turns into refinement.

You're not reacting.

You're choosing.

I went through this process and realized that a lot of what I thought was necessary was just unexamined. It had become part of my life without being re-evaluated. Once I started questioning it, I found areas where I could reduce without feeling like I was giving anything up.

In many cases, the opposite happened.

Things became simpler.

Cleaner.

Less demanding.

That's the outcome you're looking for.

Not deprivation.

Efficiency.

Because every reduction in required income increases your flexibility. It creates margin that didn't exist before. It gives you room to think, to adjust, to make decisions without everything being tied to maintaining the same level.

And that margin compounds.

As your required income drops, your Zeronaire Ratio improves. As your ratio improves, your decisions become less constrained. As your decisions become less constrained, your life starts to open up.

That's how the system works.

You don't need extreme changes.

You need consistent ones.

Each reduction moves you forward.

Each adjustment creates space.

And over time, that space becomes something you feel.

Not just in your numbers.

But in how you live.

Section 3: Rebuild

Elimination creates space.

Reduction expands it.

But neither of those matter if you don't **rebuild correctly**.

Because if you remove and reduce without changing how your structure is designed, the old patterns come back. The system rebuilds itself, just in slightly different forms. New obligations replace old ones. The baseline creeps back up. And before you know it, you're back in a structure that requires more than you intended.

That's why this phase matters.

This is where you build a foundation that actually supports you.

Not one that depends on you.

Rebuilding starts with a simple shift in mindset.

You're no longer asking, "What can I afford?"

You're asking, **"What does my life need to operate well without creating pressure?"**

That's a different standard.

Because now you're designing intentionally.

You start with your baseline.

What does your life cost after elimination and reduction? What does it require at a level that feels stable, not stretched? This becomes your new foundation, and the goal is to keep it controlled.

Not minimal.

Controlled.

Because control is what gives you flexibility.

From there, you begin to build stability into your system.

That means creating margin, not just temporarily, but structurally. You allow for variability. You account for changes. You create a setup that can absorb disruption without immediately tightening around you.

This is where most people skip steps.

They focus on cutting, but they don't focus on stabilizing.

And without stability, any progress feels temporary.

I learned this the hard way.

There were times I reduced aggressively, created space, and felt like I had momentum. But because I didn't rebuild with intention, the same patterns reappeared. The structure slowly expanded again, and I found myself maintaining more than I planned.

That's when I realized something important.

If you don't redesign your system, it will default back to what it was.

Rebuilding also means changing how you approach growth.

You don't automatically expand your lifestyle when income increases. You don't immediately take on new obligations just because you have the capacity. You evaluate whether something deserves a place in your structure based on how it affects your required income and your flexibility.

That's how you protect what you've built.

You create a system where income can grow, but your required income stays controlled. Where you can take advantage of opportunities without increasing your dependency. Where your structure supports your decisions instead of limiting them.

That's the goal.

Not just to remove pressure.

But to build something that doesn't recreate it.

And when you get this right, something shifts.

You stop feeling like you're managing your life.

You start feeling like your life is working for you.

That's what rebuilding does.

It turns temporary progress into something sustainable.

And once you have that, everything else becomes easier.

Because now you're not constantly correcting.

You're operating from a foundation that supports the direction you actually want to go.

Chapter 20: The Zeronaire 90 Day Reset

Section 1: Phase 1: Awareness

Most people never truly pause long enough to see their life clearly.

They adjust, react, and try to improve things while everything is still in motion, but they rarely step back and examine the full structure they're operating within. Because of that, even well-intentioned changes tend to stay at the surface, and the underlying system remains untouched.

That's why nothing fundamentally shifts.

The 90 Day Reset begins with something different.

It begins with a deliberate pause, not from responsibility, but from autopilot.

This phase is about creating distance between you and your normal patterns so you can observe them without immediately reacting. Because real clarity doesn't come from assumptions or quick estimates. It comes from seeing how your life actually operates in real time, without filtering it through what you think should be happening.

For the first 30 days, your role is simple, but not easy.

You track everything.

Every dollar that comes in and every dollar that goes out. Every recurring expense, every variable purchase, every decision that adds to or reinforces your current structure. The goal is not perfection, and it's not judgment. The goal is accuracy.

Because most people are operating from an incomplete picture.

They underestimate what they spend, overlook how often certain decisions occur, and assume things are under control simply because nothing has forced a correction yet. Tracking removes that layer of assumption and replaces it with something far more valuable.

Evidence.

But this phase is not just about numbers.

It's about behavior.

You begin to observe when you spend, what triggers it, and how those decisions connect to your environment, your emotions, and your routines. You start to notice patterns that were previously invisible because they were happening automatically.

Maybe it's convenience. Maybe it's stress. Maybe it's simply habit. Whatever it is, you begin to see how often your structure is being reinforced without a conscious decision being made.

That realization changes things.

Because once you see a pattern clearly, you can no longer pretend it isn't there.

I went through this process myself and realized something that caught me off guard. I wasn't just maintaining my structure, I was actively reinforcing it on a daily basis. Small decisions, repeated consistently, were keeping everything exactly as it was, even when I thought I was trying to improve it.

That's the power of this phase.

It brings everything into focus.

You begin to understand not just what your life costs, but how it continues to cost it. You see where the pressure is coming from, what's increasing your required income, and what's quietly keeping it elevated.

And once you have that level of clarity, something shifts.

You don't need to guess what to do next.

You don't need motivation or external advice.

You know.

Because control doesn't start with action.

It starts with understanding.

And this phase is where that understanding begins.

Section 2: Phase 2: Control

Once you see everything clearly, the next step is not to overhaul your life overnight.

It's to take control of it.

This is where most people make a mistake. They move too fast. They try to cut everything, fix everything, and force a new structure immediately. For a short period of time, it feels productive. There's momentum, there's energy, and it feels like real change is happening.

But it doesn't hold.

Because intensity is not the same as control.

Phase 2 is different.

This is where you begin to **intentionally reshape your structure**, using the clarity you built in Phase 1. You're no longer guessing where the pressure is coming from. You know exactly what's driving your required income, and now you start addressing it in a way that is deliberate and sustainable.

The first priority is stabilization.

You stop making decisions that increase your required income. No new destructive debt. No new obligations that your future has to carry. This alone creates an immediate shift, because for the first time, your structure is no longer expanding.

It's contained.

From there, you begin to reduce.

Not randomly.

Strategically.

You target the areas that have the most impact on your required income and your flexibility. The fixed expenses that repeat every month. The obligations that are consuming your future time. The patterns you identified in Phase 1 that are quietly reinforcing your structure.

You don't eliminate everything.

You remove and adjust what matters.

Because this phase is about control, not restriction.

I approached this differently than I had in the past.

Instead of reacting emotionally, I treated it like a system. I looked at each obligation and asked what it required from me over time. Not just whether I could afford it, but whether it deserved a place in my life based on what it was costing me in time and flexibility.

That shift changed how I made decisions.

Because once you connect each expense to your future time, it becomes much harder to justify things that don't actually improve your life.

This is also where behavior starts to change in a meaningful way.

You begin creating space between impulse and action. You pause before committing to something new. You evaluate decisions based on their structural impact, not just their immediate benefit.

That pause is powerful.

Because it interrupts the patterns that built your current system.

Over time, these adjustments start to compound.

Your required income begins to drop. Your obligation load starts to lighten. Your decisions become more intentional. And as those changes take hold, you start to feel something that may not have been there for a while.

Relief.

Not because everything is fixed, but because your life is no longer moving in the wrong direction.

It's stabilizing.

And once your structure is stable, you can actually begin to build something better.

That's what this phase is about.

Taking what you've seen and turning it into control.

Not through extreme action.

But through consistent, intentional decisions that reshape how your life operates.

Because once you have control, everything that comes next becomes possible.

Section 3: Phase 3: Freedom

By the time you reach this phase, something important has already happened.

You've created control.

Your structure is no longer expanding without your awareness. Your required income has started to come down. Your decisions are more intentional, and for the first time, your life is not being driven purely by what it demands from you.

That alone changes everything.

But this phase is where you take it further.

Because control creates stability.

Freedom comes from what you do with it.

Phase 3 is about **optimization and protection**. You're no longer focused on fixing problems. You're focused on building a structure that gives you flexibility, protects your time, and allows you to operate by choice instead of obligation.

This is where the Zeronaire identity starts to take hold.

You begin to look at your life differently.

Not in terms of what you can afford, but in terms of what your life requires to function well without creating pressure. That becomes your anchor. And once you have that anchor, every decision starts to get filtered through it.

Does this increase my required income?

Does this reduce my flexibility?

Does this deserve a place in my life?

Those questions become automatic.

That's the shift.

Because now you're not reacting.

You're designing.

This is also where you start to optimize how your income works for you.

Not by chasing more for the sake of more, but by aligning it with your structure. You create margin intentionally. You allow income to grow without allowing your required income to follow. You build systems, investments, or opportunities that increase your flexibility instead of your dependency.

That's where leverage starts to work in your favor.

But just as important as optimization is protection.

Because once you create space, you have to protect it.

That means resisting the pull to expand unnecessarily. It means not defaulting back to old patterns when income increases or when things feel stable again. It means maintaining the discipline to keep your structure controlled, even when you have the capacity to grow it.

I've seen how easy it is to lose this.

There were times when things were working, when income was strong and pressure was low, and the temptation to expand was always there. It didn't feel like a mistake in the moment. It felt like progress.

But expansion without intention always comes with a cost.

And that cost shows up later.

What I learned is that freedom is not something you achieve once.

It's something you maintain.

Through decisions.

Through awareness.

Through discipline that doesn't feel restrictive, but aligned.

Because once you experience what it feels like to have control over your time, even in small ways, it changes what you value. You begin to prioritize space over excess. Flexibility over status. Control over accumulation.

That's when the identity fully shifts.

You're no longer trying to become a Zeronaire.

You're operating like one.

Your structure supports you. Your decisions reinforce your freedom. Your life is no longer built around what it demands, but around what you choose to allow into it.

That's the outcome of this phase.

Not perfection.

Not unlimited wealth.

But something far more valuable.

A life that gives you back your time.

And once you have that, you realize that was the goal all along.

PART VI – THE ZERONAIRE LIFESTYLE: Living with Freedom

Chapter 21: Designing a Low Dependency Lifestyle

Section 1: Fixed Cost Control

If you want freedom to last, it has to be built into your structure.

Not occasionally.

Consistently.

And the biggest factor that determines whether your life stays flexible or slowly tightens again comes down to one thing.

Your fixed costs.

These are the commitments that show up every month whether you think about them or not. Housing, transportation, insurance, recurring services, anything that requires payment without a decision being made.

They define your baseline.

They determine what your life costs to exist before you make a single choice.

And because they repeat, they carry more weight than anything else.

That's where control has to start.

Most people don't design their fixed costs.

They inherit them.

They make decisions in the moment based on what feels right or what they can afford at the time, and over time those decisions become permanent. What started as a choice becomes a requirement, and once it becomes a requirement, it stops being questioned.

That's how dependency builds.

Quietly.

Incrementally.

Until your life requires more than you ever intended.

I've lived this.

There were points where my fixed costs were high enough that everything else in my life had to adjust around them. It didn't matter how much I earned, because the baseline was already set. The system required a certain level of income just to stay in place.

That's not control.

That's maintenance.

The shift happens when you start designing your fixed costs with intention.

You begin asking different questions.

Not "Can I afford this?"

But **"What does this commit me to?"**

Because every fixed cost is not just a payment.

It's a claim on your future time.

And once you look at it that way, your decisions change.

You start favoring flexibility over maximum capacity. You choose options that give you room instead of options that push your baseline to its limit. You avoid locking yourself into structures that require constant output just to maintain.

That doesn't mean living small.

It means living controlled.

There's a difference.

A low dependency life is not about minimizing everything.

It's about making sure nothing owns you.

Because when your fixed costs are controlled, everything else opens up. Your required income drops. Your Zeronaire Ratio improves. Your decisions become less constrained, and your life starts to feel lighter in a way that's hard to explain until you experience it.

That's the foundation.

Not more income.

More control over what your life requires.

And once you build that into your structure, you don't have to chase freedom.

You're already operating inside it.

Section 2: Smart Living Decisions

Most of your financial life is not shaped by big, one-time decisions.

It's shaped by a handful of **core lifestyle choices** that quietly define everything else.

Where you live.
What you drive.
How you structure your day-to-day life.

These decisions don't just impact your expenses.

They set your baseline.

And once that baseline is set, everything else adjusts around it.

That's why this matters more than people realize.

Because you don't feel the weight of these decisions all at once. You feel them over time, as they shape what your life requires to function. They determine how much income you need, how flexible your schedule can be, and how much room you have to make changes when you want to.

I've seen this play out clearly.

Two people can earn the same amount of money and live completely different lives, simply because of how they structured these core decisions. One builds a life that requires constant output to sustain, while the other creates space without sacrificing what actually matters.

The difference is not income.

It's design.

Housing is usually the biggest lever.

It's also the one people are most emotional about.

It's easy to stretch here. To justify more space, a better location, a higher-end option, because it feels like a reflection of success or stability. And in the moment, it often makes sense.

But housing is not just a place you live.

It's one of the largest commitments you make.

It sets the tone for everything else.

When that commitment is too high, it raises your required income in a way that's hard to unwind. It locks you into a certain level of output, and that pressure carries into every other decision you make.

Transportation works the same way.

Cars are one of the easiest places for people to overextend, because the payment makes it feel manageable. But that payment is not isolated. It becomes part of your baseline, and over time, it contributes to a structure that requires more than it should.

The key is not avoiding these decisions.

It's approaching them with clarity.

You start asking whether each choice supports the life you want to build or whether it simply looks good in the moment. You evaluate how each decision affects your required income, your flexibility, and your ability to adjust if your priorities change.

That's what makes it a smart decision.

Not just that you can afford it.

But that it aligns with your structure.

I've made both types of choices.

There were times I optimized for appearance, convenience, or what felt like progress, and those decisions came with a cost that showed up later. There were also times I chose differently, where I prioritized flexibility and control, and those decisions created space that I could actually use.

That contrast is what changed how I approach everything now.

Because once you understand that a few key decisions define your entire structure, you stop treating them casually.

You treat them like what they are.

Foundational.

And when you get those right, everything else becomes easier.

Your required income stays controlled.

Your flexibility stays intact.

And your life is no longer built around what it demands, but around what you choose.

Section 3: Financial Simplicity

Complexity is expensive.

Not just financially, but mentally.

The more accounts you have, the more payments you're tracking, the more moving pieces your life depends on, the harder it becomes to maintain control. Things get missed. Decisions get rushed. You spend more time managing your life than actually living it.

And most of that complexity isn't necessary.

It builds slowly.

A new subscription here. Another account there. Multiple credit cards, scattered payments, overlapping services, things added for convenience that eventually become part of your baseline. None of it feels significant on its own, but over time it creates a system that's harder to see and even harder to control.

That's where simplicity becomes powerful.

Not because it's minimal.

Because it's clear.

A simple financial structure allows you to see exactly what's happening at any given time. You know what your life requires. You know where your money is going. You know what decisions are being made and why.

That clarity reduces friction.

And when friction goes down, control goes up.

This doesn't mean eliminating everything.

It means **streamlining what matters**.

Fewer accounts that actually serve a purpose. Fewer recurring charges that you don't actively value. A structure where income flows in, obligations are clear, and nothing is hidden behind layers of complexity that require constant attention to manage.

I didn't always operate this way.

There were times where my financial setup was spread across multiple systems, accounts, and commitments. It worked, but it required constant oversight. If I didn't pay attention, things slipped. Not in a catastrophic way, but enough to create unnecessary stress.

Once I simplified it, everything changed.

Not dramatically.

But noticeably.

Decisions became easier because there was less noise. I didn't have to think as hard about where things stood. I could see it clearly, which meant I could act quickly and intentionally when needed.

That's the real benefit.

Simplicity creates visibility.

And visibility creates control.

It also creates something else.

Capacity.

When your system is simple, it requires less from you to maintain it. Less time, less energy, less attention. That capacity can then be used elsewhere, in ways that actually move your life forward instead of just sustaining it.

That's what most people are missing.

Not effort.

Clarity.

Because when your financial life is simple, you're not constantly reacting.

You're operating with awareness.

And when you combine that with controlled fixed costs and intentional decisions, you create a structure that doesn't just function.

It supports you.

That's what a Zeronaire lifestyle looks like.

Not complicated.

Not overwhelming.

Just clear, controlled, and built in a way that gives you your time back.

Chapter 22: Using Leverage for Freedom

Section 1: The Right Kind of Debt

At this point, you're no longer trying to escape debt.

You're trying to **use it correctly**.

That's an important shift.

Because the goal of this book is not to convince you that all debt is bad. It's to make sure you understand exactly what it's doing in your life before you take it on.

And when used the right way, debt can actually support the very thing you're building.

Freedom.

But only if it meets a very specific standard.

The right kind of debt does one of three things.

It **produces income,**
it **reduces your required income,**
or it **creates an asset that increases your flexibility over time.**

If it doesn't do one of those, it's not helping you.

It's just adding weight.

This is where most people get it wrong.

They take on debt for things that feel productive, or feel justified, but don't actually change their structure in a meaningful way. The result is more obligation without more control, which is the exact opposite of what you're trying to build.

When leverage is used correctly, it changes the equation.

Instead of your income supporting your obligations, the asset begins to support them. That shift, even if it starts small, is what creates momentum toward freedom.

For example, if you take on debt to acquire something that generates consistent income, and that income exceeds the cost of the debt, you've created positive movement. Your required income doesn't increase in the same way, because the asset is carrying part of the load.

That's leverage working for you.

Or if you use capital to build something that gives you more control over how you earn, whether that's a business, a system, or a capability that reduces your reliance on a single income stream, you've increased your flexibility.

That's leverage working for you.

But this only works if you stay disciplined.

Because leverage amplifies outcomes.

If the decision is strong, it accelerates your progress.

If the decision is weak, it accelerates your dependency.

There's no neutral.

I've experienced both sides of this.

There were times I took on obligations that didn't produce anything meaningful, and they tightened my structure more than I expected. There were also times where I used capital intentionally, and those decisions created space that didn't exist before.

The difference wasn't the tool.

It was the intent and the outcome.

That's what you have to stay focused on.

Not whether something is called an investment.

But whether it actually improves your position.

Because at this stage, every decision should be aligned with one objective.

More control over your time.

And the right kind of debt, when used carefully, can help you get there faster.

Section 2: Risk vs Reward

Leverage only works when you respect the risk that comes with it.

That's where people get into trouble.

They focus on the upside. The potential return. The opportunity to accelerate progress. And all of that is real. Leverage can move things forward faster than almost anything else.

But it can also move things backward just as fast.

That's the part that has to stay front and center.

Because every time you take on leverage, you're making a trade.

You're trading certainty for potential.

And whether that trade makes sense depends on how well you understand both sides.

The reward side is easy to see.

Additional income. Increased flexibility. The ability to build something that reduces your dependence on a single source. When it works, it can change your position quickly and meaningfully.

The risk side is quieter.

It shows up in what happens if things don't go as planned. If the income doesn't materialize. If the asset underperforms. If the timeline stretches longer than expected. If external factors shift in ways you didn't anticipate.

That's where leverage gets dangerous.

Not because it exists.

But because it was taken on without fully accounting for those possibilities.

I've been in situations where something looked solid on paper. The numbers worked. The logic made sense. But the margin for error was too thin, and when things didn't go exactly as planned, the pressure showed up immediately.

That's what leverage does.

It exposes your structure.

If you're already tight, it tightens you further.

If you have space, it becomes something you can manage.

That's why risk is not just about the deal.

It's about your position.

Before taking on leverage, the question is not just whether the opportunity is good.

It's whether your structure can absorb it if it doesn't go perfectly.

Do you have margin?

Do you have flexibility?

Do you have the ability to carry it without it immediately increasing your dependency?

Those questions matter more than the projected return.

Because returns are uncertain.

Structure is real.

The goal is not to avoid risk completely.

It's to take **controlled risk**.

Risk that is understood.

Risk that is sized appropriately.

Risk that, even if it doesn't work as expected, does not put you back into a position where your life is driven by obligation instead of choice.

That's the balance.

Leverage should move you closer to freedom, not further from it.

And the only way that happens is if the downside is something you can live with, not something that forces you into a position you were trying to escape in the first place.

When you approach it that way, your decisions change.

You become more selective.

More disciplined.

More focused on alignment than opportunity.

And that's what keeps leverage working for you instead of against you.

Section 3: Freedom-Oriented Investing

Most people invest for one reason.

To make more money.

And there's nothing wrong with that.

But if your goal is to become a Zeronaire, the objective shifts.

You're not just investing for returns.

You're investing for **freedom**.

That's a very different lens.

Because now the question is not, "What gives me the highest return?"

It's **"What gives me the most control over my time?"**

Those are not always the same thing.

There are plenty of investments that look great on paper. High potential returns, strong growth, impressive upside. But if they come with volatility that forces you to stay locked into a high-income structure, or if they require constant attention and stress to manage, they may not actually move you closer to what you're trying to build.

They might even do the opposite.

That's why freedom-oriented investing is about alignment.

Not just performance.

You start prioritizing investments that either produce consistent income, reduce your dependency, or give you optionality. Things that contribute to your structure in a way that makes your life easier to manage, not harder.

Consistency starts to matter more than intensity.

Reliability starts to matter more than maximum upside.

Because what you're really building is a system that supports your life without requiring constant effort to maintain it.

I had to learn this shift.

There was a time when I chased growth for the sake of growth. Bigger returns, faster movement, more aggressive strategies. And while some of those worked, they didn't always translate into more control. In some cases, they created more pressure, because they required me to stay engaged at a level that didn't actually give me the flexibility I was after.

That's when I started looking at things differently.

I began asking whether an investment actually improved my structure.

Did it reduce what I needed to earn?

Did it create income I could rely on?

Did it give me more options, or did it just increase my exposure?

That changed everything.

Because once you evaluate investments through that lens, a lot of things that look attractive lose their appeal. And other things, things that may seem less exciting on the surface, start to stand out because of what they actually do for your life.

This doesn't mean you avoid growth.

It means you align it.

You choose opportunities that fit within your structure instead of forcing your structure to support them. You build in a way that allows you to step back over time, not one that requires you to stay fully engaged just to keep everything working.

That's the goal.

To create a system where your investments contribute to your freedom instead of competing with it.

Because at the end of the day, the return that matters most is not just financial.

It's control.

Control over your time.

Control over your decisions.

Control over how you live.

And when your investments support that, you're not just building wealth.

You're building a life that actually works for you.

Chapter 23: The Freedom Dividend

Section 1: Time Ownership

This is where it starts to feel real.

Not on paper.

Not in theory.

In your actual day.

The Freedom Dividend is what you get back when your life stops requiring everything from you. And the first place you feel it is in your time.

Not more hours.

More control over how those hours are used.

Most people don't realize how little control they actually have until they experience what it feels like to have it. Their schedule is shaped by obligations, deadlines, payments, expectations, and responsibilities that were built over time. Each one made sense when it was added, but together they create a structure that dictates how their days unfold.

That's not ownership.

That's response.

When your required income is high and your obligations are fixed, your time is already allocated before the day even begins. You don't wake up and decide how you want to spend your time. You wake up and execute what your life requires to stay in place.

I've lived that.

And I didn't question it at first, because it felt normal. It felt productive. It looked like progress from the outside. But internally, there was always a sense that my time wasn't fully mine.

That changes when your structure changes.

As your required income drops and your flexibility increases, your schedule starts to open. Not all at once, but gradually. You begin to notice that you're not reacting to everything the same way. You have space to think, to choose, to decide how you want to spend your time instead of immediately defaulting to what's required.

That's the shift.

You move from managing your time to owning it.

And ownership doesn't mean doing nothing.

It means having the ability to decide.

You can still work hard. You can still build. You can still pursue ambitious goals. But now it's driven by choice, not necessity. You're not doing it because your structure demands it. You're doing it because you've decided it's worth your time.

That difference is everything.

Because once you experience even a small amount of time ownership, your priorities begin to change. You start to value space. You protect it. You become more selective about what you allow to take your time, because you understand what it costs to give it away.

Time becomes intentional.

Not scheduled for you.

But chosen by you.

That's the first dividend.

And once you feel it, you realize it was more valuable than anything you were trying to accumulate before.

Section 2: Career Flexibility

For most people, their career is not a choice.

It's a requirement.

Not because they don't have skills or opportunities, but because their financial structure doesn't allow for anything else. Their income isn't just something they earn. It's something their entire life depends on continuing without interruption.

That creates pressure.

Not always obvious, but constant.

It shows up in the decisions people don't make. Staying in roles longer than they should. Avoiding risks that could lead to something better. Accepting situations that don't align, simply because walking away is not an option.

That's not a career.

That's a dependency.

I've been there.

From the outside, everything can look successful. Good income, strong role, forward momentum. But internally, you know that stepping away, even temporarily, would create immediate stress. That realization changes how you operate, whether you acknowledge it or not.

Because when your life depends on your income, your career starts to control you.

That's what shifts as you move toward a Zeronaire structure.

As your required income decreases and your flexibility increases, your relationship with work changes. Not because you stop caring, but because you're no longer forced to make every decision based on maintaining the same level.

You gain options.

You can step away from situations that don't make sense. You can explore different paths without immediate pressure. You can take calculated risks that were previously off the table because your structure couldn't absorb them.

That's career flexibility.

Not the absence of work.

The presence of choice.

You're no longer locked into a single path just to sustain your life. You can adjust. You can pivot. You can decide where your time and energy are best used, instead of defaulting to what your structure demands.

That doesn't mean everything becomes easy.

It means everything becomes intentional.

I noticed this shift gradually.

Decisions that used to feel heavy started to feel lighter. Not because they didn't matter, but because they weren't tied to immediate survival. I could evaluate opportunities based on alignment, not just stability. I could think longer-term without everything being filtered through short-term necessity.

That's when work starts to feel different.

You're no longer working to maintain your life.

You're working because it aligns with what you want to build.

That's a completely different experience.

And it changes how you show up.

Because when you're operating from choice instead of pressure, your decisions improve. Your focus improves. Your ability to create, lead, and build improves, because you're not constantly managing the weight of dependency in the background.

That's the second dividend.

The ability to choose your work, instead of being controlled by it.

And once you have that, your career stops being something you endure.

It becomes something you direct.

Section 3: Mental Clarity

There's a level of noise that comes with financial pressure that most people don't even realize they're carrying.

It becomes normal.

Constant background calculations. Thinking about what's due, what's coming up, what needs to be maintained. Running through scenarios in your head, even when you're not trying to. It doesn't always feel like stress in the traditional sense.

It just feels like life.

But it's not neutral.

It's weight.

And over time, that weight affects how you think, how you make decisions, and how you show up in everything you do.

When your structure requires a certain level of income to stay in place, your mind is always working to protect it. Even when things are going well, there's an underlying awareness that everything has to continue. That awareness shapes your behavior in ways that are easy to overlook.

You become more reactive.

More cautious.

More focused on maintaining than exploring.

I didn't fully recognize how much of that I was carrying until it started to go away.

As my required income dropped and my structure became more controlled, something shifted that had nothing to do with money directly.

The noise quieted.

Not completely.

But enough that I could feel the difference.

Decisions became clearer because they weren't being filtered through constant pressure. I wasn't running everything through a lens of "what happens if this disrupts my structure?" That question used to sit in the background of almost every decision, even if I didn't say it out loud.

When that pressure lifted, my thinking changed.

I could focus longer.

I could evaluate things more objectively.

I could step back and actually think instead of constantly reacting.

That's mental clarity.

Not just less stress.

More space.

Space to think, to create, to make decisions without everything being tied to maintaining the same level of output.

And that space compounds.

Because when your mind is not occupied with constant maintenance, you start to use it differently. You think more strategically. You see opportunities more clearly. You make decisions that are aligned instead of reactive.

That affects everything.

Your work improves.

Your relationships improve.

Your ability to actually enjoy what you've built improves.

This is one of the most overlooked parts of financial freedom.

People focus on what they can buy, what they can do, where they can go.

But they underestimate what it feels like to not carry that constant pressure.

To not have your mind tied up in what has to happen next just to keep everything in place.

That's the third dividend.

Clarity.

And once you experience it, you realize it's not just a benefit.

It's a completely different way to live.

Chapter 24: The Zeronaire Life

Section 1: Living Intentionally

At some point, everything simplifies.

Not because life becomes easy.

But because you become clear.

You're no longer reacting to what your life demands. You're no longer making decisions just to maintain a structure that was built over time without full awareness. You've stepped out of that cycle, and now you have something most people never fully experience.

Choice.

That's what living intentionally actually means.

Not having endless options.

Having the ability to choose what matters and let the rest go.

When your structure is controlled, your required income is stable, and your time is not fully committed before the day begins, your decisions start to come from a different place. You're no longer asking what you have to do.

You're asking what's worth doing.

That shift changes everything.

You begin to look at your time differently. You stop filling it automatically. You become more selective, not out of restriction, but out of clarity. You understand that every commitment you make carries weight, and you choose carefully what deserves a place in your life.

I've experienced this transition.

There was a point where I stopped trying to optimize everything and started focusing on alignment. What actually mattered. What I wanted my time to go toward. What was worth building, and what was simply noise that had accumulated over time.

That's when things started to feel different.

Not faster.

Not bigger.

Better.

Because when you're living intentionally, you're not constantly pulled in different directions. Your decisions start to align with each other. Your time, your energy, and your focus begin moving in the same direction instead of being scattered across things that don't actually matter.

That creates a level of consistency that most people never reach.

Not because they don't want to.

Because they don't have the space to think that way.

Intentional living requires room.

Room to think.

Room to choose.

Room to say no.

And that's what this entire system has been building toward.

Not just financial change.

Clarity.

Because once you have that clarity, your life stops feeling like something you're managing.

It starts feeling like something you're directing.

And that's the foundation of the Zeronaire life.

Section 2: Experiences Over Status

There's a shift that happens when you stop trying to prove something.

Not to other people.

To yourself.

A lot of financial decisions early on are tied to perception. What something looks like. What it signals. What it says about where you are in life. The house, the car, the upgrades, the visible markers that make it feel like you're progressing.

And for a while, that can feel good.

It gives you feedback.

It gives you validation.

But it also comes with a cost that most people don't fully connect.

Because those decisions are rarely isolated.

They become part of your structure.

And once they do, they start requiring something from you.

That's where the tradeoff happens.

You gain status.

But you give up flexibility.

I've made those decisions.

Things that looked right, felt right, and on the surface made sense. But over time, I started to realize that a lot of what I thought I was gaining wasn't actually improving how I lived. It was improving how things looked.

That distinction matters.

Because once your structure is under control, your priorities begin to shift naturally. You stop needing external validation in the same way, because your life no longer depends on maintaining a certain image.

You start valuing something else.

Experiences.

Not in the sense of constant travel or spending for the sake of doing more, but in terms of how you actually spend your time. What you're doing, who you're with, and whether those moments feel aligned with what matters to you.

That's where real value starts to show up.

A simple day where you control your schedule can feel better than something expensive that comes with pressure attached to it. Time with people you care about, without distraction or obligation, starts to carry more weight than things that are designed to be seen.

That's the shift.

From external to internal.

From appearance to experience.

It doesn't mean you stop enjoying nice things.

It means they're no longer the point.

They become optional.

And when something is optional, it stops controlling you.

I noticed this in a way I didn't expect.

The more control I had over my time, the less interest I had in things that only added to my structure without improving my life. It wasn't forced. It just stopped being appealing in the same way.

Because once you experience what it feels like to have space, to have control, to have your time aligned with what you actually care about, it becomes harder to trade that for something that only looks good from the outside.

That's what this section comes down to.

Redefining success.

Not by what's visible.

But by how your life actually feels.

And when you make that shift, your decisions follow.

You stop building a life that needs to be maintained.

And start living one that you actually want to experience.

Section 3: Sustaining Freedom

Getting to freedom is one thing.

Keeping it is something else entirely.

Because the same forces that built your old structure don't disappear. They're still there. The pull to upgrade, to expand, to take on more because you can. The quiet justification that comes with higher income or lower pressure. The belief that "this time it's different."

That's how people drift back.

Not all at once.

Gradually.

A new obligation here. A higher baseline there. Small decisions that feel harmless in isolation, but over time start to rebuild the same structure you worked to change.

That's why sustaining freedom requires something most people don't expect.

Not effort.

Awareness.

Because once you've created a low dependency structure, your job is no longer to fix things.

It's to **protect what you've built**.

That starts with remembering what actually creates your freedom.

Not your income.

Your **required income**.

As long as that stays controlled, you have space. The moment it starts creeping up without intention, your flexibility begins to shrink, even if your income is increasing at the same time.

That's the trap.

It doesn't feel like a step backward, because everything still works.

Until it doesn't.

I've seen how easy it is to let this happen.

There were moments where things were stable, income was strong, and the pressure was low. That's when the temptation shows up. To take on more, to upgrade, to expand because it feels like progress.

And sometimes it is.

But only if it's intentional.

Because expansion without awareness always carries a cost, and that cost shows up later in the form of reduced flexibility.

That's what you have to guard against.

Sustaining freedom is not about staying static.

It's about staying intentional.

You can grow. You can build. You can increase your income and your capabilities. But you do it in a way that doesn't rebuild the same dependency you worked to remove.

That means continuing to use the same filter.

Does this increase my required income?

Does this reduce my flexibility?

Does this align with how I actually want to live?

Those questions don't go away.

They become part of how you operate.

That's what keeps you aligned.

Over time, this becomes less about discipline and more about identity.

You don't have to force yourself to avoid certain decisions.

They just stop making sense.

Because once you've experienced what it feels like to have control over your time, to have space in your life, to not be driven by constant obligation, you're not willing to trade that away easily.

That's the difference.

Freedom stops being a goal.

It becomes your standard.

And when it becomes your standard, sustaining it is no longer something you have to think about constantly.

It's how you live.

CONCLUSION

Section 1: The Final Reframe

Most people think wealth is about how much you make.

That's the story.

Increase your income, upgrade your life, accumulate more, and eventually you'll reach a point where everything feels secure. That's what we're taught, and for a while, it seems true. More income creates more options, more comfort, more visible progress.

But there's a problem with that model.

It ignores what your life actually requires.

Because if your income grows and your lifestyle grows with it, nothing really changes. You're still dependent on maintaining that level. You're still trading your time to support a structure that now costs more than it did before.

It just looks better while you're doing it.

That's the part most people miss.

They think they're building wealth, but they're really building **obligation**.

And obligation has a cost that doesn't show up on a balance sheet.

It shows up in your time.

In your decisions.

In what you can't do, even if you have the money to do it.

I've lived both sides of this.

There was a point where income was strong, things looked successful, and everything appeared to be moving in the right direction. But underneath it, the structure required that income to continue. The margin wasn't as wide as it seemed, and the flexibility wasn't what I thought it was.

That realization changes how you see everything.

Because once you understand that **required income** is the real driver, not just income itself, the entire equation shifts.

You stop asking how much you can make.

You start asking how much your life needs.

And more importantly, whether that number is working for you or against you.

That's the reframe.

Wealth is not income.
Wealth is control over your time.

If your life requires everything you earn, you don't have control.

If your structure allows you to choose how you spend your time, you do.

It's that simple.

And once you see it clearly, your priorities begin to change.

You stop building a life that needs constant support.

You start designing one that supports you.

You begin to value flexibility over appearance, space over excess, control over accumulation. You realize that the goal was never just to earn more, it was to create a life that doesn't require you to constantly maintain it.

That's what a Zeronaire understands.

It's not about having less.

It's about needing less to live the way you actually want.

And once that clicks, everything changes.

Not because your income disappears.

But because it stops being the thing your life depends on.

Section 2: The Choice

Now that you see it, you can't unsee it.

You understand how the system works. You see how income, spending, and obligations connect. You recognize how small decisions compound into a structure that either gives you flexibility or slowly takes it away.

That awareness changes something.

Because once you know, it becomes a choice.

Not a one-time decision.

A series of decisions.

You can continue on the default path.

Earn more, upgrade your lifestyle, take on new obligations, and maintain a structure that looks successful but requires constant output to sustain it. That path is familiar. It's reinforced everywhere you look. Most people around you are on it, and from the outside, it often looks like progress.

There's nothing unusual about it.

But there is a cost.

Your time becomes committed. Your decisions become constrained. Your flexibility narrows, even as your income increases. You build a life that works, but only as long as you keep working at the same level to support it.

Or you can choose a different path.

You can choose to build a life that does not depend on everything you earn. A life where your required income is controlled, your obligations are intentional, and your structure gives you room instead of pressure.

That path is less visible.

But it's real.

And it doesn't require a dramatic change.

It requires direction.

I didn't make this shift all at once.

It happened through a series of decisions that, on their own, didn't seem significant. Choosing not to expand when I could. Removing something that didn't need to be there. Questioning whether a decision improved my structure or just added to it.

Each one created a little more space.

And that space changed how I operated.

Because once you experience even a small amount of flexibility, you start to see what's possible. You begin to recognize how much of your life was being shaped by what it required instead of what you wanted.

That's when the decision becomes clear.

Not easy.

But clear.

Because at that point, you're not choosing between working and not working.

You're choosing between **dependency and control**.

Between a life that demands and a life that allows.

And the truth is, no one is forcing that decision.

Not your job.

Not your income.

Not your circumstances.

Your structure is built through your choices.

And it can be rebuilt the same way.

One decision at a time.

In one direction or the other.

That's the choice.

And now, you're aware of it.

Section 3: The Zeronaire Identity

At the beginning, this was about money.

Now it's about identity.

Because once you understand how your life is structured, and once you start making decisions differently, something deeper begins to change. You don't just manage your finances differently.

You start to **operate differently**.

That's what defines a Zeronaire.

Not a number.

Not a net worth.

A way of thinking.

A way of deciding.

A way of living that prioritizes control over accumulation and intention over impulse.

You stop seeing money as the goal.

You start seeing it as a tool.

A tool to create space. A tool to reduce dependency. A tool to give you more control over how you spend your time.

That shift changes how you evaluate everything.

You become aware of your **required income** at all times. You understand what your life actually needs, and you protect that number. Not out of fear, but out of clarity, because you know that as long as it stays controlled, your flexibility stays intact.

You begin using a filter without even thinking about it.

Does this increase my required income?
Does this reduce my flexibility?
Does this align with how I want to live?

Those questions become automatic.

That's when you know the identity has shifted.

Because you're no longer forcing discipline.

You're operating from alignment.

I've experienced this change.

There was a time when decisions were driven by growth, by momentum, by what felt like progress. And while that created results, it also created a structure that required constant attention to maintain.

Now, the approach is different.

I still build.

I still push.

But I do it within a structure that I control.

That's the difference.

Because a Zeronaire doesn't stop striving.

They stop building a life that depends on constant output to sustain itself.

They build a life that gives them options.

That gives them space.

That gives them the ability to choose how they spend their time without everything being pre-committed.

That's the identity.

And once it becomes part of how you operate, you don't think about going back.

Because you've seen both sides.

You've experienced what it feels like to maintain a structure.

And you've experienced what it feels like to control one.

And once you've felt that difference, even in small ways, you don't measure success the same way anymore.

You don't measure it by how much you have.

You measure it by how much you **don't need** to live the way you want.

That's what it means to be a Zeronaire.

Section 4: The Zeronaire System (Beyond the Book)

This book gives you clarity.

But clarity alone doesn't change your life.

It shows you the structure. It helps you see where you are, how you got there, and what needs to shift. But if nothing follows that awareness, your old patterns will eventually take over again.

That's not a lack of discipline.

It's a lack of system.

Because without a system, change depends on motivation.

And motivation doesn't last.

That's why everything you've read is designed to connect to something bigger.

The Zeronaire System.

Not as a concept.

As a repeatable way to operate.

The assessment you completed is not just an exercise. It's a way to continuously evaluate your structure. The score is not just a number. It's feedback that shows you whether you're moving toward more control or drifting back into dependency.

The playbook is not a one-time fix.

It's a process.

Eliminate what works against you.
Reduce what your life requires.
Rebuild in a way that supports you.

And the 90 Day Reset is not just a reset.

It's a model you can return to whenever your structure starts to shift or expand beyond what you intended.

Because it will.

That's the reality.

Life changes. Income changes. Opportunities show up. And without something to anchor you, it's easy to slowly rebuild the same dependency you worked to remove.

The system prevents that.

It gives you a way to stay aligned without having to rethink everything from the beginning every time.

I didn't have this fully defined early on.

I had pieces of it. I made adjustments, learned through experience, corrected when things drifted. But once I started treating it like a system instead of a series of decisions, everything became more consistent.

More controlled.

More intentional.

That's the difference.

Because this is not something you do once.

It's something you operate within.

You revisit it. You refine it. You use it to make decisions, to evaluate opportunities, and to ensure that your life continues moving in the direction you've chosen.

That's how freedom is sustained.

Not through one breakthrough moment.

Through a structure that supports you long after the initial change.

If you want to go deeper, apply the system in real time, and track your progress, everything is built out at ZeronaireLife.com.

The full assessment, scoring tools, and system framework are there to help you turn this from an idea into something you actually live.

So this is not the end.

It's the starting point.

You now have the awareness.
You have the framework.
You have the system.

What matters now is how you use it.

Because this only works if it becomes part of how you operate.

And when it does, something shifts.

You stop trying to manage your life.

You start running it.

Section 5: Final Close

You don't need more.

You've been told that you do.

More income. More upgrades. More accumulation. More of everything that looks like progress from the outside. And for a while, that belief drives you forward. It keeps you moving, building, chasing the next level.

But at some point, if you're paying attention, you start to realize something.

More doesn't always give you more.

Sometimes it gives you less.

Less flexibility. Less control. Less ownership over your time. Because every layer you add without intention becomes something your life has to support, and over time, that support turns into dependency.

That's the cycle.

And breaking it doesn't require you to stop building.

It requires you to build differently.

The truth is simple.

Your life expands when your requirements shrink.

Not when your income increases.

When what you need becomes controlled.

That's where space comes from.

That's where flexibility comes from.

That's where control begins.

I didn't find this by chasing less.

I found it by realizing that everything I was building came with a cost that didn't always show up immediately. And once I started paying attention to that cost, my decisions changed. Not all at once, but consistently enough that my structure began to shift.

And when it did, everything else followed.

My time felt different.

My decisions felt different.

My life felt different.

Not because I had more.

Because I needed less to live the way I actually wanted.

That's what this has been about the entire time.

Not eliminating ambition.

Not avoiding success.

Redefining it.

So before you move on, there's one question worth asking yourself.

Not what do you want to earn.

Not what do you want to have.

What does your life actually require?

Because that answer determines everything.

It determines how much you need to work.

How much flexibility you have.

How much control you actually possess.

And once you're clear on that, you have a choice.

To continue building a life that depends on you.

Or to design one that works for you.

You don't become a Zeronaire when you have more.

You become one when you **need less to live the way you want**.

And once you understand that, you realize something most people never do.

Freedom was never out of reach.

It was just buried under everything you thought you needed.

About the Author

Paul Szyarto has spent more than two decades building businesses, leading organizations, and operating at the intersection of technology, strategy, and execution. His career spans roles as a CEO, enterprise architect, and transformation leader, working with global companies across industries including manufacturing, utilities, construction, and technology.

Alongside his corporate leadership, Paul has built and scaled multiple entrepreneurial ventures across technology, artificial intelligence, and private equity. His financial success was not the result of a single path, but the combination of both corporate leadership and entrepreneurial execution, giving him a unique perspective on how wealth is built from multiple angles.

He holds a Juris Doctorate, an MBA from Oxford University, and a Master's in Program and Project Management, and is completing a PhD in Business with a focus on Applied AI. Over the course of his career, he has led large-scale initiatives, built high-performing teams, and developed systems supporting billions of dollars in enterprise operations.

From the outside, it looked like success.

And in many ways, it was.

Paul reached a level of financial success that most people spend their lives chasing. Income was strong. Opportunities were abundant. The trajectory, both in corporate leadership and entrepreneurial ventures, reflected everything conventional success is supposed to represent.

But underneath it, something didn't add up.

The more he earned, the more his life required. The higher the income, the more the structure expanded alongside it. Expectations increased. Commitments grew. And with it came a quiet but constant pressure to maintain, sustain, and continue at that level.

More had created a need for more.

That realization changed everything.

Income, growth, and achievement do not automatically create freedom. When not designed intentionally, they can do the opposite. They can create a structure that demands constant output, leaving little room for flexibility, clarity, or control over time.

That realization became the foundation for Zeronaire.

Through personal experience, hard lessons, and years of observing how people build and maintain financial structures, Paul developed a different perspective on wealth. One that prioritizes control over accumulation, simplicity over complexity, and time over status.

Zeronaire is not a theory.

It is a system built from lived experience.

Today, Paul continues to operate across multiple ventures while applying the principles outlined in this book. His focus is not just on building businesses, but on designing a life that maintains flexibility, protects time, and operates by choice rather than obligation.

He lives this philosophy with his family, grounded in the belief that true success is not defined by how much you have, but by how much control you have over how you live.

Learn more about Paul Szyarto at: www.paulszyarto.com

If this book resonated with you, the next step is simple.

Go to: **www.zeronairelife.com**

Take the assessment.

Calculate your score.

Start the reset.

This is where the system becomes real.